BONSAI DESIGN

JAPANESE MAPLES

BONSAI DESIGN

JAPANESE MAPLES

PETER D. ADAMS

Sterling Publishing Co., Inc.   New York

This book is dedicated to my family.

ACKNOWLEDGEMENTS

I am indebted to Jonathan Harrison for the creative photography throughout the book, and to Dan Barton for the winter and summer images of Trees no. 10 and 12.

All line drawings are by the author.

AUTHOR'S NOTE

I have tried as far as possible to relate my experiences generally to seasons rather than months. My use of months has been dictated broadly by the cycle of the plant's life. I hope people in the Southern Hemisphere will find the conversion chart acceptable and take the text as an indication of timings.

SOUTHERN HEMISPHERE		NORTHERN HEMISPHERE
Mid-summer =	January	= Mid-winter
Late summer =	February	= Late winter
Early autumn =	March	= Early spring
Mid-autumn =	April	= Mid-spring
Late autumn =	May	= Late spring
Early winter =	June	= Early summer
Mid-winter =	July	= Mid-summer
Late winter =	August	= Late summer
Early spring =	September	= Early autumn
Mid-spring =	October	= Mid-autumn
Late spring =	November	= Late autumn
Early summer =	December	= Early winter

UK/USA CHEMICAL EQUIVALENTS

UK	USA
GHF	Blood, fish and bone meal
TEF	Metl-Frit tm (glass composition)
Phostrogen	Miracle-Gro tm (plant food)
Tomato Feed	0:10:10
Chempak No 2	Ra-Pid-Gro tm (grass fertilizer)
Benomyl	Benlate tm (fungicide)

Published in 1988 by
Sterling Publishing Co., Inc.
Two Park Avenue,
New York, N.Y. 10016

ISBN 0–8069–6902–4

First published in Great Britain in 1988 by Unwin Hyman as 'Bonsai Design: The Japanese Maple'.

Published by arrangement with Unwin Hyman Limited, London.

This edition available in the United States, Canada and the Philippine Islands only

Printed in Italy

Designed by Colin Lewis

Contents

Profile of Japanese Maples

NATURAL HABITAT AND PLANT DESCRIPTION

Acer Palmatum, the Japanese Maple, has a wide distribution and grows at many elevations throughout its native habitat. In cultivation, it is seen everywhere as a garden plant and as a bonsai.

Under good conditions the tree grows to 3–15 m (9–14 ft) in a spreading or rounded, open-tiered shape, depending on cultivar. Light woodland conditions affording some shade and wind protection are necessary if the tree is to achieve its ideal form.

Young trees are strongly ascendant and multi-trunked in form. The branches tend to follow this shape when young, and later either become more horizontal, or send out many sub-branches which assume flattish positions and lend the tree the typically layered appearance.

There is much variation in height and spread, but common to most cultivars is the palmate leaf form and dense foliage mass. The leaf commonly has five or more lobes, and is usually toothed along the margin, often with deep divisions between lobes. The colour and size of the leaf varies enormously but the strains favoured for bonsai usually have leaves of between 3–5 cm (1–2 in) in spread, with a base colour of bright green edged with red, borne on deep red leaf stalks or petioles.

The seasonal foliage colour on such strains is usually interesting, and ranges from pinkish orange and lettuce green in the spring, which gives an overall subdued browny appearance like washed blood, to the summer colour of deep green, to the bright reds and yellows of autumn. The winter form consists of a periphery of reddish twigs, borne on apple green branches, sometimes bloomed with blue, springing from the trunk, which deepens to buff. The buff colour is a transitional stage and, as the tree ages, this is replaced by whitish grey, thicker bark, often striped with buff.

There are countless variations within the type, and none of the large trees imported into the UK as bonsai have ever proved identical, thus indicating they were developed from collected material or from seed. It is only where cultivars are propagated vegetatively that the standard plant emerges. Of course, from the bonsai point of view the natural hybridization often results in a very desirable plant, which it then becomes necessary to propagate vegetatively, by cuttings, grafting or layering, in order to maintain and increase the new clone. It is only by these means that the clone will 'come true', in any quantity, as seed is notoriously variable. Currently, for example, I propagate from Maple stock that came from Japan ten years ago. This clone has leaves which are about 2.5 cm (1 in) in spread and are of good colour throughout each season. The twig colour is deep red and there is early bark formation. The clone is not botanically distinct, and is unnamed, but by sheer chance, has all the right attributes for bonsai.

CULTIVARS OF THE JAPANESE MAPLE

RED LEAVED CULTIVARS
Some of the most attractive are those Maples that produce bright crimson spring foliage. There are two groupings, both attractive in subtly different ways: *Seigen* and *Beniseigai* are more feathery and in the full spring phase are red in general appearance; *Chishio* and *Deshojo* have broader leaf lobes and are a blue red by comparison in the same period. Horticulturally, *Seigen* and *Beniseigai* are softer in the spring than the other two. All red leaved cultivars need spring protection until the first set of leaves has hardened.

ROUGH BARKED CULTIVARS
As the name suggests, these varieties have a bark texture that adds a further dimension of 'age' to their general appearance, which otherwise follows the Maple type. The two most famous cultivars in this group are the Pine Bark Maple, *Itsusai Nishiki*, which has vertical, winged bark resembling *Pseudoacacia*, and the Rough Bark Maple, *Arakawa*, which has a warty bark resembling *Kalmia Latifolia*. The Pine Bark Maple is not really winter hardy, and needs greenhouse protection.

DWARF CULTIVARS
There are also genetic dwarfs of the Japanese Maple which lend themselves particularly well to bonsai culture. Among such dwarf strains, which resemble the witches broom pine cultivars in their miniature aspect, are well known strains such as *Kyohime*, *Kashima*, and an older cultivar known as *Yatsubusa*.

All these varieties have myriads of tiny leaves and twigs, elegant branches and dainty trunks, and firm looking roots. Whereas most of the time the job of the bonsai grower is to build leaf density in Maples, with these dwarf cultivars deep grooming is often necessary to open the canopy of leaf, and even to cut holes! However, the true beauty of these trees is in their winter form. The sense of scale deriving from the sum of all these tiny features makes a truly proportional and a compellingly beautiful bonsai image.

When training the dwarf cultivars remember they tend to be base dominant like azaleas. Undue basal shooting or strength should be redirected by pruning and thinning these areas. This will redirect energy towards the apex, which with these species, particularly *Kyohime*, is the weakest area.

ACER BUERGERANUM
The Trident Maple is not exclusively Japanese, but for the purposes of this

book has been included under the same grouping.

The tree makes about 10 m (32 ft) in height and is generally upright rather than spreading. Young trees have apple green and buff coloured bark that later silvers before darkening. The bark on old trees is dark grey, brown, or even blackish and often there are fissures of bright orange inner bark. Some squarish flaking of the outer bark can give quite a textured appearance.

The leaves are three-lobed with blue reverse and dark green upper sides. There is great variation in the leaf formation. Those trees with straightish, clean-cut leaves, usually display good autumn colour. The leaf size as bonsai is typically reduced to between 1.5–2.5 cm (0.5–1 in).

The apple green, buff to grey coloured shoots, twigs and branches are very pleasing in their fine appearance and produce masses of leaves. The trunk is strong and rugged, and the root structure of this tree is very pleasant too and flattens on the soil surface, becoming so broad it often appears to spread the trunk line right across the soil. The winter form, with the powerful trunk balanced by densely twigged branches and a webbed root system, is very appealing. The constant leaf pinching practised on this species reduces the size of the leaf substantially and produces a most wonderful autumn colour.

The comments on the horticultural preferences of Japanese Maples hold good for the Trident Maple. Generally, the Trident Maple is much tougher than the Japanese Maples, except for its root system which is fleshy and thus susceptible to frost, unlike the finer and more wiry Japanese Maple. However, the root system of the Trident Maple may be significantly improved in texture if the system of soil mixtures, watering, feeding and placement that I developed to counter severe winters is followed. This helps correct its one great weakness and makes it far more reliable in a pot.

HORTICULTURAL PREFERENCES AS BONSAI

SOIL

Japanese Maple bonsai grow best in a light, well drained soil, with lots of sand. A well composed sand consisting of sharp and round particles between 2–4 mm (0.07–0.15 in) in size, mixed with some organic matter is excellent for the main soil, with 4–6 mm (0.15–0.23 in) for the lower soil and main drainage course. The mixture should have a preponderance of round sand as roots pass rapidly through round sand which encourages gentle growth patterns. If sharp sand predominates there will be more divisions and aberrations in the tree, as the root tips become sliced and divided. There is a very real relationship between the nature of branch and root systems, and, with most deciduous trees, placing the accent on round sand particles will encourage the formation of flowing branch patterns. Some sharp sand is obviously desirable to encourage variation in branch patterns but the proportion is low, about 80 per cent round sand and 20 per cent sharp should be ideal.

While most of the Japanese Maple cultivars will grow in a wide range of mediums *if* aeration and drainage are good, they perform best in a mixture that favours about 60 to 70 per cent sand to 40 to 30 per cent organic material. The organic soil components are leaf mould (screened and rotted oak and beech are best) and peat.

A mixture that works well is (parts by volume):

    6 parts sand
    2 parts leaf mould
    2 parts peat

Ensure all ingredients are dry and sieved carefully. I remove all material finer than 1 mm (0.04 in). Mix thoroughly and grip-test the mixture: it should feel like gritty sponge, with little adhesion. The use of loam is likely to prove a problem in wet climates, particularly over winter, whereas lighter soil holding less water will freeze less and thus avoid excessive damage to the root system. Over the 84/85 winter where temperatures in the United Kingdom dropped to −25°C, only Maples growing in the traditionally recommended mixtures based on Japanese recipes were damaged. (A typical recipe would incorporate up to 7 parts of loam or red soil.) It will also be found that *all* Maples when grown in the lighter mixture develop a very much *finer* root system which winters safely.

The reason that heavy soils do not suit root growth in the United Kingdom is because of our wet winters, and heavy soils such as Japanese red subsoil hold too much moisture during dormancy. The Japanese winter is essentially dry by comparison and so the growers there do not encounter the problems of root rot caused by waterlogged soil when exposed to winter rainfall. So remember, do not use imported red soil if you wish your tree to survive.

WATER

Keep the Japanese Maple evenly moist. You will find the recommended soil is light and drains fast and the use of a screen to shade sunlight and reduce wind passage will compensate for the minor inconvenience of drying and will help conserve moisture. The rapid percolation of water and air obtained with this mixture helps produce sound roots and strong, healthy top growth.

There are fewer differences in the amounts of water given to evolving and completed Maples than with some bonsai. Of all the cultivars mentioned, it is mandatory to remember that the dwarf types *must* remain moist. If *Kyohime* dries out, because the tree is so strongly base dominant, the apex of the tree will be lost. The reason for this is that these trees are very sensitive and need water distributed evenly throughout their systems. If this supply is interrupted, the tree tends to shed its weaker points, so ensure that these species are adequately protected at all times.

Obviously, young evolving material needs ample water; those plants in the structural state need less and the maturing plant requires still less. The divisions between the stages are less marked than with, say, the Scots Pine, and in all cases, the plant must *never* go short of water.

With the exception of young material that is being grown for trunk girth where 'mass makes wood', and water application is liberal, it is sensible to move other plants to a location where air circulation, sunlight and a sensibly reduced watering regime will all help monitor the extending internodal branch length. Young material will also benefit from the increase in ventilation but here the rule is water plentifully.

Trees that are well watered bud back strongly when pruned and have round, plump wood that withstands winter cold. Special sensitivity occurs after repotting, when after the initial watering in, care should be taken to

Stage 1

Plants in development. Generous water encourages vigour.

JAN	FEB	MAR	APR	MAY	JUN	JUL	AUG	SEP	OCT	NOV	DEC
Damp	Damp	Moist	Moist	Moist	Moist	Moist	Moist	Damp	Damp	Damp	Damp

Stage 2

Plants in structure and refinement. Watering is used to stabilize growth and encourage shorter nodes.

JAN	FEB	MAR	APR	MAY	JUN	JUL	AUG	SEP	OCT	NOV	DEC
Damp	Damp	Moist	Moist	Damp	Damp	Damp	Moist	Damp	Damp	Damp	Damp

Stage 3

Between May and July the trick is to ensure that the plant remains damp, but to avoid too many inundations that produce sappy growth. If the *relative* dryness is difficult to obtain on your site with safety, consider increasing the wind and sun protection to a point where the plant loses less moisture through its leaves.

avoid wetting new shoots and leaves unduly. If the leaves are heavily wetted in early spring, the soggy, clinging foliage becomes vulnerable to various leaf spot disorders.

Great care should be taken with the maintenance of ventilation between the initial and subsequent soil waterings. Raise plants off any surface that impedes air passage beneath the pot. When shallow or long containers are used, be especially cautious with the amounts of water given, as water does tend to collect in these. Other units requiring special care at all times are those arrangements with stone, as these retain a lot of moisture. All Maples are susceptible to root rot and therefore it is a sensible precaution to keep the soil dryish until the roots take hold. This usually takes about a month. If the roots can be nursed along and the first set of leaves kept scrupulously healthy, the tree will soon produce an overall background of leaf, and then normal watering may be applied. Later, evening foliage spray during the summer will benefit the tree in all cases.

The tree's location will also dictate the amounts of water required. Hot and windy weather is disastrous to Japanese Maples if they are unprotected. That first set of healthy leaves must be protected until it becomes leather hard to the touch, and then, and only then, can it safely be assumed that further new shoots will not be damaged.

Watch particularly for strong winds where the red leaved cultivars are concerned. If they sustain damage this will show as blackening of the leaf and shoot. If this occurs, move the affected plant to a well ventilated, shaded structure such as a shaded greenhouse or poly-tunnel and maintain soil water. Unless it has been recently repotted, the tree may also be fed lightly. The increased humidity and light feeding will soon repair the damage, even to the soft leaved *Beniseigai* cultivar. This procedure holds good for all leaf damaged Maples. If recently repotted trees become leaf burnt, they must not be fed, but will benefit both from the application of Vitamin B1 root stimulant and the greenhouse environment.

When autumn colour is desired

this may be encouraged to some extent by a slight increase in the amounts of water given in mid to late summer. Watering should be even and adequate at this time, and followed by a dryer regime from late summer into mid autumn. The summer watering helps maintain the leaves in a smooth, unscorched condition and then the dryer soil of the next phase, together with the onset of lower night temperatures, combine to seal the sugars in the leaves and to give deep autumn colours. If the summer moisture levels go on into autumn, colours are often disappointing as the sugars tend to be utilized. Equally, if colours are uneven among a collection of Maples, it usually means that those colouring well are more root bound, and hence less active and dryer than those with greener leaves. In the United Kingdom, if summer rains blending with autumn rains threaten to inhibit the formation of good colour, it is worth using overhead plastic to maintain the damp soil condition independently of the weather.

TRANSPLANTING

Japanese Maples are easy to transplant.

STANDARD REPOTTING

Follow usual bonsai procedures employing the recommended light soil mix. Take about a third to half of the root mass, depending on the vigour of the tree. The more vigorous trees will benefit from the additional pot space that pruning provides and the deeper thinning will encourage further root development close in to the trunk. Periodic removal at each repotting of alternate slices of soil will also keep the root system lively. This is normally only carried out on well established trees with a defined root pad.

REPOTTING FREQUENCY

Once every three years is sufficient for young to middle aged trees—those between three and twenty years old. Older trees quite probably can go to four or more years and will grow better if not disturbed too frequently. The decision to repot depends on observation of the root ball's density and its ability to hold moisture and drain properly. Indeed, as trees age, or as the design matures, it is inadvisable to repot frequently as this encourages strong, coarse growth. With the older plants, the periodic 'cake slice' removal and limited soil change will assist in preserving the delicacy of twigs and branches. Young plants, on the other hand, usually have their roots washed off, and are pruned and then replanted with the maximum of new soil mixture to promote vigorous development.

Root bound trees are often a problem to keep damp as the water can barely penetrate the mass. Equally, if lack of drainage occurs with a tree that previously drained well, you must repot in order to avoid root rot.

If there is a problem with the roots that has gone unnoticed, some dessication of the branches and trunk will occur. This shows up as fissured wrinkling running in parallel lines along the limb. Under these circumstances the best thing to do is to regard the tree as a huge cutting. Prepare a large box raised on bricks for ventilation, and fill it with a very open sandy soil. Wash the root system off and cut away rotted root areas. Steep the tree in a solution of Vitamin B1 root stimulant overnight and then plant it in the sandy mixture. The provision of greenhouse conditions, with extra humidity, will help. Spray the top of the tree with Benomyl and Liquid Copper

Fungicide. Try to water the soil with Vitamin B1 solution when it starts to dry, but be careful not to over water.

If the treatment is successful, the tree should respond and send out leaves in about a month. The timing of this procedure is ideally in early spring but if soil collapse happens in other seasons the tree may be treated in this way if the leaves are removed first. The tree will need at least a year of careful treatment after such trauma.

REPOTTING DWARF CULTIVARS

The dwarf cultivars are easy to repot. If branch pruning is planned, remember to cut the roots first to prevent weeping. There are full notes following this section on the relationship of branch pruning and repotting.

As the branch system is dense, the root system is equally so. This means that, in addition to the standard one third removal of soil and root mass, the 'cake slice' removal is also a good way to revitalize the root system and admit air to the inner portions.

REPOTTING THE TRIDENT MAPLE

The Trident Maple is easy to repot. If the light soil composition has been used, a firm, compact root system may be expected. This makes a pleasant contrast to the gelatinous mess that used to greet the grower using loam soils after a winter of frost and rain.

If the roots are evenly distributed, the root mass may be combed outwards, beginning at a point one third of the way in. This will usually expose a collar of root that encircles the pot and which should be unravelled and cut short. The rest of the root mass is tidied in the usual way and any strong roots may be removed in favour of lighter growth. Remove about half the amount of root that

you would with the Japanese Maple.

Branches may be trimmed back at this time to maintain a balance if deep root pruning is carried out. In a normal repot, the annual autumn tidying and grooming of branches will maintain sufficient balance above and below.

THE RELATIONSHIP OF BRANCH PRUNING AND REPOTTING

Where heavy branch reduction is planned in those years when transplanting becomes necessary, the two may be safely combined if the following sequence is observed.

Always repot the tree dry and do not water until branch pruning is complete. Carry out a regular repot but instead of watering in immediately, delay this until all undesired branches are cut and the wounds sealed. When all pruning is completed and *all* wounds are sealed, the tree may be watered in. This sequence prevents weeping. It is vital to remember with all types of Japanese Maple to seal cuts made in the spring. Trident Maples are usually more forgiving in this respect when grown in cooler latitudes. I have however seen Trident Maples from warmer areas pumping sap at an alarming rate because their roots were not cut prior to branch pruning.

The alternative to this sequence, which I use in those years when transplanting is not scheduled and pruning to redesign the branches is still desired, is that of 'paint pruning'. This, as the name implies, is a simple method by which an identifying dab of paint is applied instead of a scissor cut before the buds break. At this time the bare branches are easily selected and the redundant, dab coded material, can be safely taken off in mid season without the risk of bleeding. One simply lifts the leaves until the paint marks show up. Use an emulsion or artist's acrylic paint of a bright colour.

The other interesting point is that after pruning and refining the cut, the area may be completely concealed with acrylic paint mixed to match the bark colour. I have also mixed this paint with artist's pastels and find this makes a very accurate colour.

CONTAINERS

The container must act as a perfect flower pot with absorbent walls and ample drainage holes.

Plants in the development stage need only wooden seed trays or larger boxes. Plants in the structural stage need containers that approximate vaguely in form to the visualized end product. Plants in the refinement stage require pots of precise form and colour.

A wide range of pot textures can complement Japanese Maple. Lately in Japan the tendency has been to display Maples in containers with a green glaze that has marked areas of black variegation. Off white and dull yellow glazes are traditional and look well, and if the glaze is thickish and trickles, it introduces a pleasant rustic feeling. A discreet blue can also be pleasing if not too loud. The 'export blue' from Japan probably does the least for any bonsai, usually being loud in hue and unbroken in pigmentation. Maple bonsai blend properly in understated rather than in strident pots.

Unglazed pots in light or mid grey and medium to dark brown also look pleasant with the lacy texture of the leaf. Regarding form, Maples 'feel' right in soft contoured pots, whilst deep containers usually defeat the floating tiers of leaves in aesthetic terms. An obvious exception to this would be with a cascade tree, but

normally most Maples are grown in containers of 5–7.5 cm (2–3 in) in depth.

Some study of established bonsai is required to recognize the indefinable, successful combination between pot and tree. If a visit to the Far East is impossible, then try at least to study as many pictures as possible. You will soon see recurring themes and solutions that work well and these will help you both to choose your pot and to style your tree.

FEEDING

GH5
This is a white granular feed formed from blood, fish and bone. It requires some moisture and warmth for bacteria to break down the granules. I have been using GH5 for over 15 years on a wide variety of trees. Maples respond well to GH5.

Dosage: 1 teaspoon per 25 cm (10 in) pot with 7.5 cm (3 in) depth.

TRACE ELEMENT FRIT (TEF)
A 'glass' (fine powder) that looks like curry powder. It supplies all the micro-nutrients needed and one application lasts for a year. This gives a greater depth of colour to the foliage.

Dosage: about $\frac{1}{2}$ teaspoon per pot. Harmless to plants.

PHOSTROGEN
A white powder that is mixed with water to form a paste and diluted to strength. May be used as a foliar feed and encourages good, steady growth.

Dosage: mix to manufacturer's directions and apply freely.

0–10–10
A deep green coloured solution that is diluted to strength. Usually 1–600 parts of water is sufficient. This is both a flowering stimulant and a

Where several feeds are mentioned during the same period, space them at least one week apart. Feeds are given when buds are *active*. Suggested schedules begin in late March, in a greenhouse bud activity might be earlier, outside, bud activity might be later.

Stage 1: years 1–4

Plants in development that need mass, this covers: seedlings, grafts, layerings, nursery stock and collected material. This schedule provides heavy growth and is used to build a tree quickly.

The letter 'F' signifies foliar feed additionally at the time of soil feeding.

	JAN	FEB	MAR	APR	MAY	JUN	JUL	AUG	SEP	OCT	NOV	DEC
GH5			1				1					
TEF			1									
PHOSTROGEN			2F	1F		1						
TOMATO			1				1	1	1			
CHEMPAK no 2				2F	2F							

Stage 2: years 5–6

Plants in structure that need localized bulking of foliage. This schedule ensures a sound, slower growth. It is used to allow the grower to regulate branch thickness and density and relate this to the trunk form.

	JAN	FEB	MAR	APR	MAY	JUN	JUL	AUG	SEP	OCT	NOV	DEC
GH5			1				1					
TEF			1									
PHOSTROGEN			1F	1F								
TOMATO			1				1	1	1			
FISH					1	1	1					
CHEMPAK no 2				2F								

Stage 3: years 6+

Plants in refinement that need maintainance. This schedule holds growth but keeps the tree lively. It allows the grower time to make minute adjustments.

	JAN	FEB	MAR	APR	MAY	JUN	JUL	AUG	SEP	OCT	NOV	DEC
GH5			1									
TEF			1									
PHOSTROGEN				1								
TOMATO			1				1	1	1			
FISH				1	1	1	1					

Feed analysis	N	P	K
GH5	6.5	7.7	5
PHOSTROGEN	10	10	27
0–10–10	0	10	10
FISH EMULSION	5	1	1
CHEMPAK no. 2	25	15	15
TEF 12% iron 4% zinc 2% boron 0.13% molybdenum			

Chempak no. 2 also contains Trace Elements

growth hardener. In combination with the light soil mixture suggested, this helps the tree over winter with less risk of die-back in hard weather. It will be found that Tomorite or other tomato feeds low in nitrogen are acceptable if diluted.

FISH EMULSION

A thick paste that is diluted to strength. It is used to maintain plant growth rather than spur unwanted growth.

Dosage: 1 tablespoon per 4.5 litres (one gallon) of water. Apply freely.

CHEMPAK FORMULA 2 LIQUID FERTILIZER

A blue powder that is mixed to a paste then diluted to strength with water. It is used to spur plants and to repair superficial damage such as that described with wind burn on young leaves. It should never be used on trees with suspect root systems but only on established plants in good health, that need extra foliage, deeper colour or back budding.

Dosage: 1 teaspoon per 4.5 litres (one gallon) of water. May be used as a foliar feed. If a plant displays a weaker branch, this area may be strengthened by foliar feeding.

Never apply feed to dry soil. Never water immediately afterwards as this dilutes the feed. Never feed trees whose roots have been disturbed or those you suspect may have sustained winter damage. Instead these should be treated with Vitamin B1 root stimulant and then in the same way as trees with wind scorched leaves.

PLACEMENT

Japanese Maples grow best in light woodland cover, so for bonsai a simulation of this proves ideal.

In hot climates, if trees are grown inside a lathe cage with Netlon or Sarlon cloth at the sides, the heat and wind can be substantially controlled. A moistened ground mulch of fir bark or an equivalent is a handy way of combatting dry conditions. Students of mine who have tried this system in hot climates report a significant improvement in plant growth.

In the United Kingdom, wind is more often the enemy than sun, but when the two combine, Maples can become dried out and burnt in less than half a day if not protected. The grower really needs to understand local conditions minutely in order to erect the most applicable type of shade: where sun and shade are at their most intense; where the prevailing wind comes from; and where rainfall, snow and frost do the most damage.

In general terms Maples are quite hardy and can be strengthened over winter by early placement in a frost shelter. The one I use is open to moderate rainfall. I feed with 0–10–10 from late summer to ripen and season the whole system of the plant and then drape polythene in front of the tree so that it is not freeze dried by sub-zero winds when the roots are frozen. Trees growing in light, dampish soil are far less affected by the cold.

I evolved this system to try to counter the effects of the severe winters experienced in the United Kingdom in the early 80s. The 84/85 winter, for example, was particularly dangerous to Maples: up to Christmas, the weather was so mild that trees were almost in leaf, and then temperatures dropped and stayed low with sub-zero winds. Under those conditions much damage would be sustained by plants growing in the traditional heavy soils, unprotected by such a system. In heavy soil the root system becomes solid with ice and the wind then dessicates the trunk and branches. The effect of such protracted freezing is to mush the root system resulting in extensive die-back of the branches or even death.

The spring placement is critical to Maples and many factors come into play. All winds and frost must be guarded against and every response must be made to local conditions. Following this, I tend to leave plants in their winter quarters until the end of May. Most plants are left in good light, under their growing benches with the polythene curtains rolled up, so that instant frost protection is at hand. The Maple grower's attention to weather forecasts in the spring tends to get paranoid. Larger trees which are inconvenient to move around I tend to leave in a well ventilated, polythene greenhouse with the ends open.

The green Mountain Maples usually leaf out without the need for too much cosseting, and can winter outside once one remembers the governing factors of temperature fluctuations and wind. Red leaved forms on the other hand, and also the dwarf leaved cultivars, really need to be well protected in winter and early spring as they are so tender. Even inside a poly tunnel, frost damage was sustained by the red leaved *Beniseigai* Maple shown on the cover. There was much blackening of young buds and shoots, but by feeding with Chempak no. 2, all damaged areas were replaced by strong growth and vigorous back buds appeared too. If it had wintered outside, the tree would undoubtedly have been lost.

During spring, summer and autumn, the Maple bonsai needs a growing location affording good light and ventilation. Be cautious of the wind and sun syndrome and do take into account any reflected heat. The light levels in dormancy need not be so high, which helps the grower protect a lot of trees in close proximity. I would certainly recommend the use of background heat during dormancy when periods of hard frost are forecast. The average poly-tunnel gives approximately 4 degrees of 'lift' over outside temperatures. Direct frost, of course, does not touch the plants and standby heating will be a necessity in the future now that winds with a chill factor of −25°C have been encountered in Southern England.

PESTS

APHIDS
These are round bulbous insects about 2 mm (0.08 in) in size. The types that infest Maples vary in colour from green to brown and black.

Symptoms: Blackish deposits of sooty, sticky honeydew are seen on

17

CHEMICAL	BRAND NAME	PEST CONTROLLED	APPLICATION
Dimethoate	Murphy's Systemic Insecticide	Aphids Scale insects	Fortnightly

When using chemicals wear a mask and goggles.

leaves, and shoot activity is impaired. These pests appear throughout the growing season, in warm winters, and when the plants are under glass. They are quite mobile.

Treatment: Systemic spray with Dimethoate is effective.

SCALE INSECTS

Flat or rounded scales look like pods, and vary from 1 mm (0.04 in) to 2–3 mm (0.08–0.12 in) in size, depending on type. They are usually a brownish colour. The females produce white egg sacks. They are quite mobile.

Symptoms: Leaves can yellow substantially in dappled areas. The scales will be found attached to the leaves. The larger types batten on to the twigs, branches and trunk. There may be some sooty deposits or slick, shiny areas like snail trails.

Treatment: Systemic spray with Dimethoate in May and again three weeks later is effective. A dormant spray is often a good insurance against scale in the wintering stages.

DISEASES

TAR SPOT

Symptoms: Large black spots with yellowy zones appear. Tar spot can occur with warm spring weather, or later in summer, when temperatures and humidity are high and the leaves ill ventilated.

Treatment: Spray with Liquid Copper Fungicide. Reduce leaf bulk by pruning to admit air. Elevate tree to encourage air circulation and do not spray the leaves when watering. Check that the soil is not soggy.

CORAL SPOT

Symptoms: Masses of pink dots, like pods, pin head size, appear first on dead timber. The danger is that live tissue can get infected leading to die-back. The fungus probably invades through dead timber killed by frost. Live branches wilt as the water vessels are choked by the fungus.

Treatment: Clean out dead areas and seal the wounds with Wound Seal containing fungicide. Remove all debris. Ventilate well and use Vitamin B1 root stimulant and a weak feed.

FROST DAMAGE

Symptoms: Branches die back, or if in leaf, puckering and crinkling of the leaf occur.

Treatment: Apply Vitamin B1 root stimulant in the spring. Feed with Chempak no. 2 once it becomes obvious through growth activity that no long term damage has occurred. Place in a poly tunnel or shaded greenhouse and ventilate well.

COLD

General low temperatures may cause very pale leaves to appear on the red-leaved varieties. If trees are moved to a lightly shaded greenhouse and are given foliar feed, this will help restore the colour. The *Yatsubusa* varieties may be treated in the same way. In general all these mentioned cultivars are best kept frost free.

CHEMICAL	BRAND NAME	CONDITION OR DISEASE CONTROLLED	APPLICATION
Copper	Murphy's Liquid Copper Fungicide	Tar spot	Every two to three weeks
Wound seal	Cut wound paste from Japan	Coral spot	Any time
Vitamin B1 root stimulant	Superthrive	Coral spot	Weekly March–September
Vitamin B1 root stimulant	Superthrive	Frost damage	Weekly March–September
Chempak no. 2	Chempak no. 2	Frost damage	Two to three applications April/May
Wound seal	Cut wound paste from Japan	Grey mould	Any time
Benomyl	Benlate	Grey mould	Fortnightly March–September
Copper	Murphy's Liquid Copper Fungicide	Damp-off	Fortnightly, ½ strength March–September

GREY MOULD
Symptoms: Die-back of shoots occurs, with patches of discolouration that carry grey, hairy mould. Be particularly careful to clean off old leaves in winter as these, if still attached, can rot and enable grey mould to attack and possibly even kill branches.

Treatment: Cut out dead shoots and seal wounds with tree paint. Spray tree with Benomyl and check watering and ventilation.

DAMP-OFF
Symptoms: This is shown by the atrophy and collapse of the seedlings at soil level.

Treatment: Apply Liquid Copper Fungicide. Attend to ventilation and be careful with watering. Remove all debris.

PRODUCTION CYCLES OVER SIX YEARS

Development of Mass: RAISING BY SEED

Appropriate for green Japanese Maple and Trident Maple (other Maple cultivars may be raised from cuttings, layerings or grafts)

YEAR 1
Japanese Maple seed is best stratified in autumn. Bury it in sand that has been dampened with a weak Benomyl solution and either place it where outside temperatures can work on it, or place it in a refrigerator until spring at a temperature of about 3°C.

In March sow the seed in trays containing a mixture of 3 parts sand to 1 part peat which has been pre-moistened by immersion in water. Drain well prior to sowing. Use drills to ensure even distribution of seed and sow by placing them individually and then scattering more sand over the top. Water lightly and place out of frost. Raise the trays on bricks so that air can pass underneath. (If this is not done the water forms puddles beneath the tray and can rot the seeds.) Spray with Benomyl solution periodically.

By April there should be good germination. Be careful to ventilate the emerging cotyledons and spray with Liquid Copper Fungicide or with Captan to avoid damp-off. Keep the trays damp but *not* soggy. Continue to watch for frosts. If the Maple seedlings grow strongly, they may be pricked out as the new growth pushes. As with cuttings, it is advisable when transplanting to remove dominant roots and to spread everything as radially as possible. Take time over this, as later it adds much quality to the tree if the spreading roots strike evenly into the soil.

Maple seedlings are transferred to half trays at this time or to clay azalea pots. Remember to raise all containers on bricks so that air can circulate underneath. Clay always breathes better, being porous, but by elevating them it is possible to improve the airflow capacity of plastic containers thereby making them much safer.

In May a little Vitamin B1 solution is applied weekly and this is followed by a diluted feed with Phostrogen three weeks or so after root disturbance. Continue to protect from frost. Check and spray for aphids. Feed with Phostrogen every ten days till the end of June, then once at the end of July. Fertilize with tomato feed at the end of August and again at the end of September.

In June and July any strong side shoots that threaten to compete with the apex are shortened to help

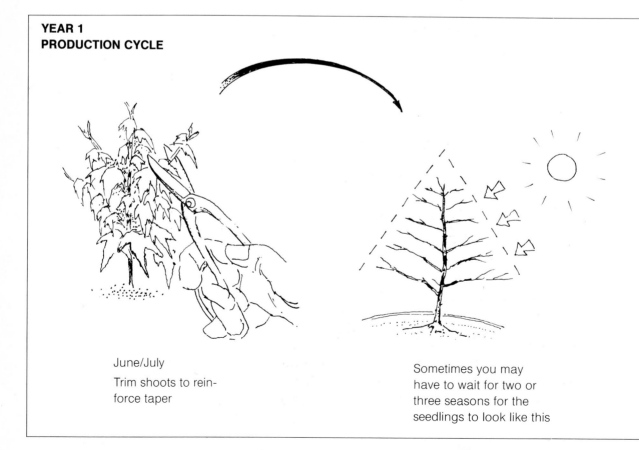

YEAR 1 PRODUCTION CYCLE

June/July
Trim shoots to reinforce taper

Sometimes you may have to wait for two or three seasons for the seedlings to look like this

maintain taper—coarse top growth tends to make trunks columnar as it swallows taper. Lower shoots are encouraged to grow unchecked to build taper—coarse lower growth tends to make the lower trunk stouter. Usually, however, trunks are tiny and unbranched at this age, but in every seed batch there will be the odd vigorous plant that may need trimming.

In August trim back any lower shoots. Check and retrim the whole tree to reinforce the conical periphery. Bear in mind that the whole suggested regime of June through August is largely theoretical and in most cases the plants will be single whips. The notes are included for those vigorous individuals which appear now and then.

In September keep plants damp. In October place in a greenhouse early after just enough frost to make the leaves turn colour and start to fall. Remove all fallen leaves in this month and November and any still attached to the plant. This is most important as this leaf tissue can become infected and kill the small plant. Spray over with Benomyl.

Development of Mass: RAISING BY CUTTINGS

Appropriate for all Maples

In March sections of previous years' wood are taken. The cuttings should be approximately matchstick thick and 5–10 cm (2–4 in) in length. Prepare seed trays with an insertion mixture of between 6 and 7 parts sand to 3 and 4 parts peat. Pre-wet the insertion mixture by standing the trays in water to almost the same depth. Wait until the surface darkens and then remove and cant the trays to drain off the surplus water.

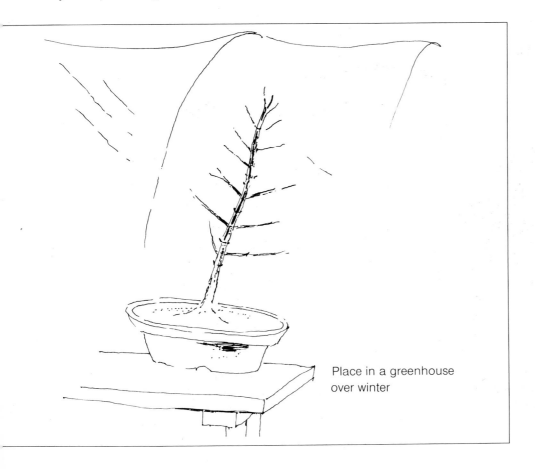

Place in a greenhouse over winter

You will need hormone rooting powder that is strong enough to root hardwood cuttings. Recut the Maple pieces using sharp clean scissors. Make the cuts square and adjacent to a node. Dip in hormone powder and insert the cuttings to a depth of at least 2.5 cm (1 in). Make sure the bottoms of the cuttings do not touch the base of the tray. Space them in rows and avoid proximity to the container wall—the cuttings need lots of air, and contact with the container tends to cramp new roots and keep them overwet, leading to root rot. Spray the tops of the cuttings with Benomyl and place the trays under ventilated and lightly humid, shaded conditions. Ensure that there is an air current beneath the trays by standing them on bricks or something similar. It is possible to lose a complete tray of rooted material through soggy soil leading to root rot.

An alternative time to take cuttings is when well grown spring shoots are just going hard at the base, usually after the growth is long enough to support 5 or 6 pairs of leaves. Pinch out the soft tips and take pieces 5–10 cm (2–4 in) in length and proceed as above, but using a weaker hormone powder.

After a month or so, when new shoot activity and a test pull or two has revealed rooting, a weak feed with tomato food is beneficial and should be given at fortnightly intervals till the end of August. Protect in a greenhouse over winter and transplant in March or April, or when buds break.

One year after rooting, the transplanted cuttings are treated by the Year 2 seedling cycle.

Development of Mass: RAISING BY SEED

Cultural methods appropriate for all other Maple species

YEAR 2
Placement
In May the trays of seedlings are placed on raised benches in a greenhouse. Keep a careful watch for frosts and ventilate well. The seedlings may be placed outside to harden up but shade from sun and wind until they are strong.

YEAR 2 PRODUCTION CYCLE

April
Plants will begin to consolidate and to throw out shoots

July to August
Trim shoots to form a cone

With trimming and feeding a dense plant is formed

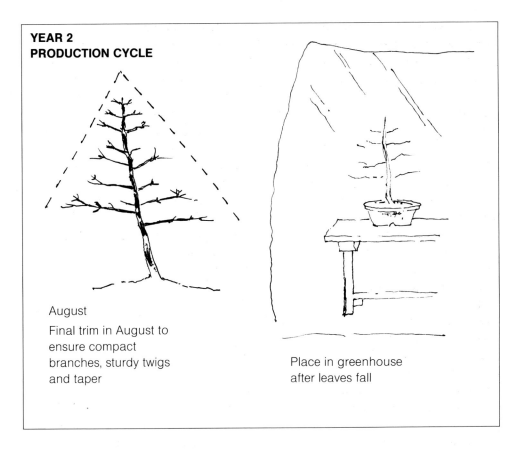

**YEAR 2
PRODUCTION CYCLE**

August

Final trim in August to
ensure compact
branches, sturdy twigs
and taper

Place in greenhouse
after leaves fall

Water
Water carefully, and as the buds
break, if the seedlings are strong, go
on to the schedule for Stage 1 (p. 20).
However, if the seedlings look weak,
some Vitamin B1 solution will prove
helpful. Keep dryish until buds are
obviously perking up.

Feeding
Ideally, Maple seedlings are fed as
their buds burst. In practice, as late
frosts may have damaged young buds,
begin by applying Vitamin B1
solution two or three times as a
stimulant to allay any possible
damage and then feed only those that
look strong. If evenly strong, then go
on to the schedule for Stage 1 (p. 20),
but at half strength.

Pests
Use the sprays suggested at half
strength, *if* aphids are present.

Shoot pruning
From April to August trim to consolidate the cone of leaves. As shoots
also spring from previously trimmed
growth, the resultant extra axillary
foliage load soon builds the seedlings
into solid little plants. Continue
trimming and feeding throughout this
period, remembering to change the
feed over from nitrogen to the tomato
type feeds (0–10–10) by mid-summer.
Give a final twig pruning in August
to arrange the tree by reinforcing the
conical form.

Protection
Place in a greenhouse from September onwards. Watch for frosts and
move the young plants before temperatures go down. They will probably be unaffected, but why take risks?

General note on year 2
The amount of lateral shoot growth

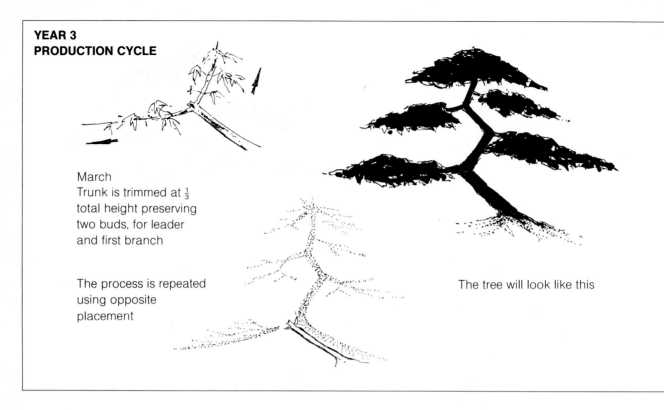

**YEAR 3
PRODUCTION CYCLE**

March
Trunk is trimmed at $\frac{1}{3}$
total height preserving
two buds, for leader
and first branch

The process is repeated
using opposite
placement

The tree will look like this

will depend very much on the growing environment and feed cycle. If there are few laterals, do not despair, they will appear next year.

Development of Mass:
RAISING BY SEED

Cultural methods applicable to cuttings
Appropriate for all Maples

YEAR 3
Placement

In March/April when the buds start to open, a decision must be made as to the desired size. In general terms, a plant destined to be 45 cm (18 in) in height is pruned at 15 cm (6 in) or so, which fixes the first branch at this height, since buds break adjacent to the cut. This enables you to develop the resulting shoots into first branch and leader. Also, this pruning helps the trunk to thicken. If the aim is to produce tiny plants, the same ratio is observed, the initial cut being made at one third of the desired height.

The yearly trimming of the leading shoot and selection of two buds for branch and leader, gives a pleasant looking tree (see diagram). Sometimes a plant may be trained with aluminium wire to curve the form substantially. When set, the branch is then trimmed back to one third and another leader trained up. By repeating this, curves are formed, and the same trunk fattening is achieved.

Such trunk wiring is usually carried out one year after root disturbance so as not to stress the tree. Trees with trunks of 3 mm (0.12 in) are safe to shape in this way. Having mentally resolved all these factors, choose and proceed to plan your tree.

If a slender, graceful tree is envisaged, then transplant the seedling into, say, a 15 cm (6 in) clay pot, or a larger plastic tray. Be careful to flatten and spread the roots so that a good, radial system is created. Trim any over-heavy roots. Use the light soil mixture and tie the plants from below to make them wind and water

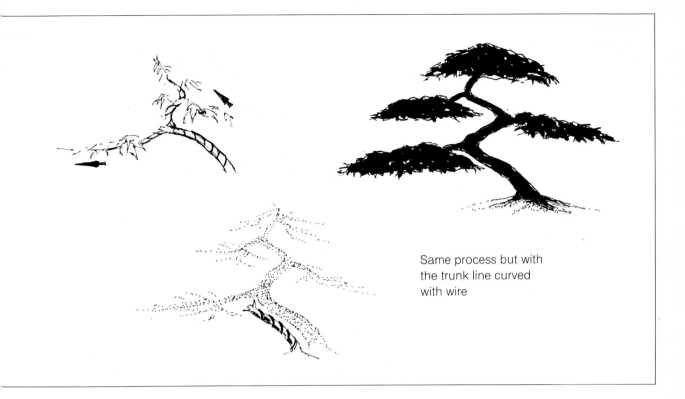

Same process but with
the trunk line curved
with wire

stable. Maintain apical form by
pinching.

   Keep transplanted trees shaded for
fast recovery. Plants will grow faster
if a ventilated greenhouse is used, but
you should harden them off by
placing them outside under light
shade during July/August.

Water
After transplanting, use Vitamin B1
solution to water in, and spray tops
with Benomyl. If buds burst strongly
the plants may be put on to the
schedule for Stage 1 (p. 20). If they
are weak-looking or slow, some more
Vitamin B1 solution will be helpful.
Keep dryish until there is improved
bud activity.

Feeding
In April/May, one month after
transplanting, if the seedlings/cuttings
appear healthy, they may be placed
on the schedule for Stage 1 (p. 20),
full strength. Those that are weak
should stay on Vitamin B1 until shoot

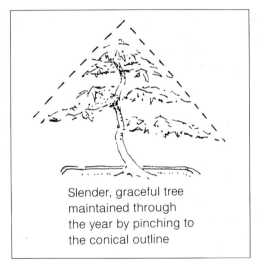

Slender, graceful tree
maintained through
the year by pinching to
the conical outline

growth is vigorous and then they can
go on the schedule for Stage 1, but at
HALF strength.

Pests
Aphids again are the main danger,
but check also for scale insects. Use
suggested sprays at half strength.

Shoot pruning
One month after transplanting if

**YEAR 4
PRODUCTION CYCLE**

Paint pruning in
February

Preserve branches
on outer bends

In June, after pruning

In June, after wiring

shoots are vigorous, the conical form is maintained by shoot pinching and the procedure is as for Year 2.

Protection
Place the plants in a greenhouse from September onwards. Watch for frosts and move the plants before temperatures drop too much.

General note
The vigour of the plant depends largely on the cultural methods employed during this year. If lateral shoots are still meagre, the use of a greenhouse environment and careful feeding in Year 4 will rectify this. With three-year-old cuttings, lateral growths will be much stronger than with those grown from seed, as the overall plant size is usually greater than that of a seedling of the same age.

Development of mass:
RAISING BY SEED

Cultural methods applicable to cuttings
Appropriate for all Maples

YEAR 4

Placement
In March when buds open, place plants on a shelf that receives good light. Protect from direct sun and wind and watch for frosts. A greenhouse will give faster development but it must be well ventilated and lightly shaded.

Water
Follow the schedule for Stage 1 (p. 20) once sound shoot development is seen.

Feeding
In March begin the schedule for Stage 1 (p. 20) once shoots are vigorous. Remember the Vitamin B1 solution technique for any which are not vigorous.

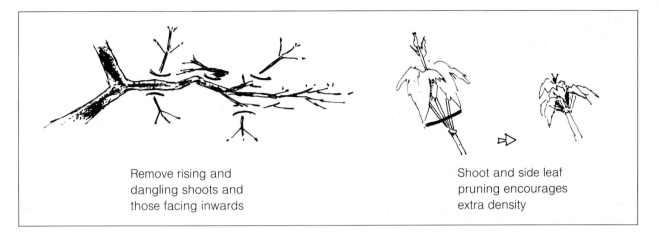

Remove rising and dangling shoots and those facing inwards

Shoot and side leaf pruning encourages extra density

Pests
Spray for aphids and scale.

Shoot pruning
Maintain conical form by pinching soft shoots. Pinch off both shoot and side leaves for extra density (see diagram).

Branch pruning
Before leaves appear, find the front of the tree (determined by the best trunk line, root placement and branch disposition) and 'paint prune'. The paint pruning system is described under Transplanting in the Horticultural Preferences (p. 13). Prune off undesired branches in June and all vertical and dangling shoots, and seal the cuts.

Wiring
Main branches are wired in June: a flat profile looks well. If trunks are to be wired, do it now.

Protection
Avoid frost contact and place on the floor of the greenhouse early.

Note on development
The period of time spent in this development phase is entirely dependent on the size and general stature of the tree envisaged. Repeat the Year 4 cycle if a compact, denser tree is required, before moving to the more specifically pruned stage of structure and form. Alternatively, the end of Year 4 is often a good time to switch to the use of a large container to enhance trunk development, perhaps linking it to Fast Trunk Development Method 2 at the three-year stage (p. 36).

Structure and form:
RAISING BY SEED

Cultural methods applicable to cuttings
Appropriate for all Maples

YEAR 5

Placement
In March place plants on a shelf that receives good light. Once again the decision for faster or slower development depends on the desired elegance or chunkiness of the image. A greenhouse will always give a faster result, with much heavier growth.

Water
Follow the schedule for Stage II (p. 11) as soon as the buds are seen to break evenly.

Feeding
In March begin the schedule for Stage II (p. 15), once bud growth is even and strong.

Pests
Spray for aphids and scale insects.

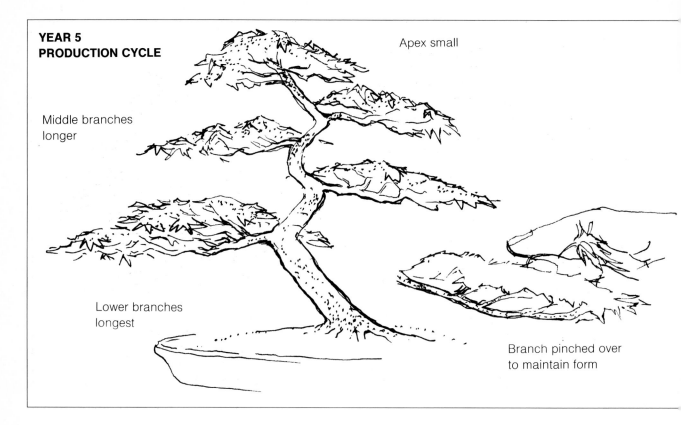

**YEAR 5
PRODUCTION CYCLE**

Apex small

Middle branches
longer

Lower branches
longest

Branch pinched over
to maintain form

Shoot pruning
Maintain shoot pinching on an overall conical shape. The apex must remain delicate and small. The lower branches will be longer but even so must be neat, so, after some healthy development, pinch back soft growth to two pairs of leaves.

Branch pruning
If any branch threatens to fatten up too much it should be pruned and a replacement twig trained into position in its place (see diagram above).

Wiring
In March, remove wire from the main branches, twigs and trunks to avoid scarring.

Protection
Avoid frost contact and protect early.

Note
The time spent in formation and structure is really determined by how much general structural disposition is still to be achieved. It is better to alternate the schedules for Years 4 and 5 until this is established, before moving to the Refinement stage of Year 6 +, where the close pinching involved to form fine detail slows down development. The decision is determined by the overall design concept.

Refinement of image:
RAISING BY SEED

Cultural methods applicable to cuttings
Appropriate for all Maples

YEAR 6 +
Placement
Transplant in March and keep in a greenhouse till May.

Water
Restore to schedule for Stage III (p. 11) when the root system has had one month to recover from transplant shock.

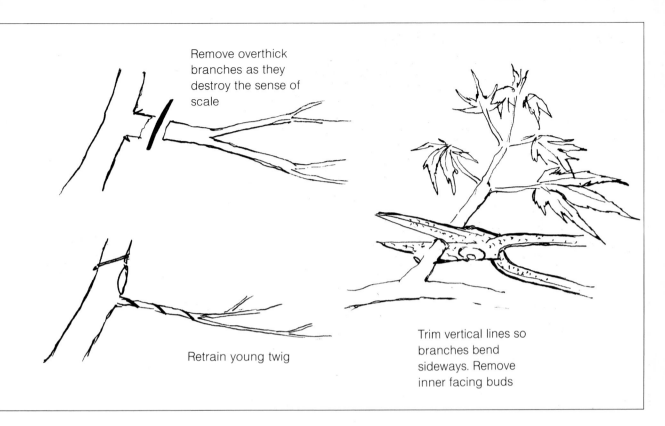

Remove overthick branches as they destroy the sense of scale

Retrain young twig

Trim vertical lines so branches bend sideways. Remove inner facing buds

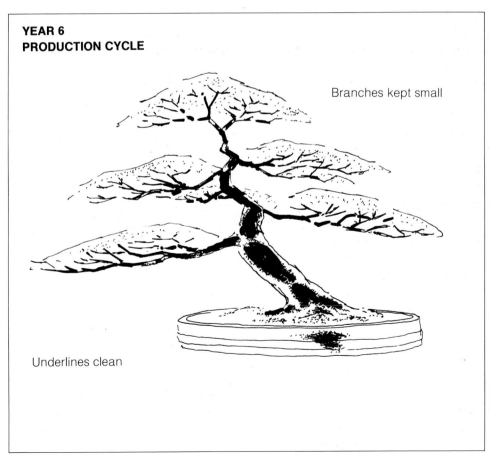

**YEAR 6
PRODUCTION CYCLE**

Branches kept small

Underlines clean

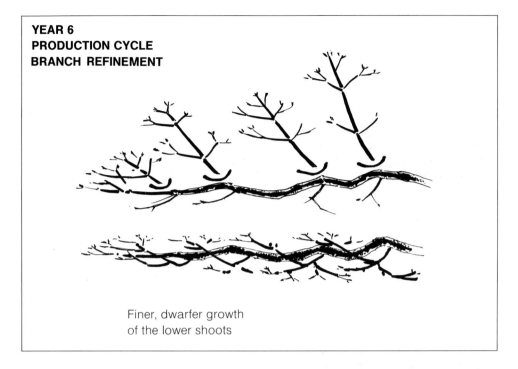

**YEAR 6
PRODUCTION CYCLE
BRANCH REFINEMENT**

Finer, dwarfer growth
of the lower shoots

Feed
Follow schedule for Stage III (p. 15)
four weeks after root disturbance.

Note on transplanting
Root prune in March and transplant
into a bonsai pot. Prune branches
back to force adventitious buds and
to arrange the form. Seal all cuts and
THEN water in. This technique is
fully explained under Transplanting.

Apart from the change for feed and
water schedules to Stage III, follow
schedule for Year 5.

**General pruning note on all
maples**
As and when the tree produces
oversize leaves, reduce the number of
these by pinching off large individuals
rather than by the process of entire
leaf stripping. Leaf stripping, whilst
effective, can stress the tree, but the
phased removal of over large leaves
achieves a significant reduction in leaf
size without harm.

Leaf cutting, or stripping, is a
process usually followed where a
quick reduction of leaf size is required. The leaves are trimmed away,
preserving the stalks to nourish the
tree, thus forcing the axillary buds
into activity. These latent shoots
produce smaller, neater leaves and the
whole process can be debilitating to
the tree. Leaf stripped trees often
tend to shed the extra branch load
during winter if selective twig thinning is not practised in the autumn.

After leaf fall, Trident Maples,
which are strong, should be tip
pruned to keep the branches compact
and full of inner bud activity.

Mountain Maples and their
Yatsubusa forms will weep if cut at
this time of the year, so these are best
pruned earlier, say in late summer.

Branch refinement
When pruning shoots in future years,
a more refined appearance and a
better sense of scale may be obtained,
if upward shoots are always removed
and the lower shoots are retained for
structure. The reason for this is that
the upper growths are sappy and the
lower growths less vigorous by
comparison, thus yielding finer twigs.

Special Techniques

FAST TRUNK DEVELOPMENT

METHOD 1

Appropriate for Trident Maples

YEAR 1

The purpose of this system is to build squat, powerful trunks, either to form low, heavy trees, or as the means to build solid bases on much bigger trees.

In March, either dig a hole about a metre (3 ft) deep or prepare a container of the same size. Mix equal parts of peat and leaf mould, and add some rotted manure and a handful or two of bone-meal and mix with the excavated soil. Then break up the soil at the bottom of the pit and refill with the mixture.

If a container is used, make sure to raise it on bricks so that air can pass beneath. If the base sits on the ground, overly wet soil can result which often leads to root rot. Do remember to site the container before filling. Use well sieved soil of the type suggested for Maples and add extra manure and bone-meal.

Select strongly growing three- to four-year-old material, and behead it at about 7.5–10 cm (3–4 in) above the root system, depending on the desired finished size, so the height of this initial cut will vary. A trunk cut at 10 cm (4 in) will ultimately yield a plant with a central trunk about 30 cm (12 in) in height and of massive taper. If a smaller plant is planned, consider making the cut at about 5 cm (2 in) above the root system. In all cases try to make the cut above a pair of buds.

Make the cut at an angle of about 30° and seal it immediately with a tree wound preparation. Try to ensure there are a number of buds left adjacent to the cut. Pruning a healthy Maple usually results in a profusion of buds.

Trim the root system lightly to even it and remove any heavy roots or twisted areas. Try to ensure that the roots spread evenly outwards. Place the tree with the roots well spread in the centre of the planting area and put an old plate or tile under the trunk area, which will encourage the

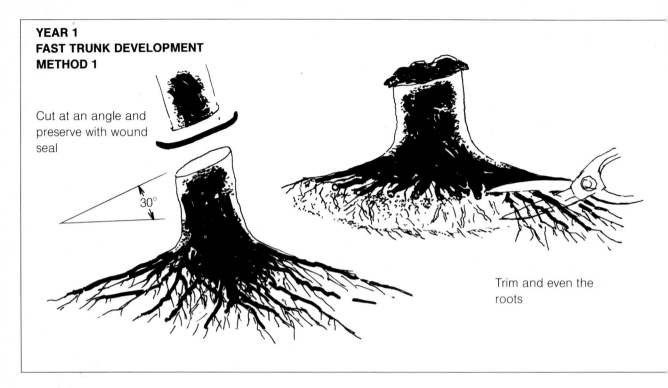

**YEAR 1
FAST TRUNK DEVELOPMENT
METHOD 1**

Cut at an angle and preserve with wound seal

30°

Trim and even the roots

formation of flat roots in the central area. Add more mixture so that the roots are well covered, but do not bury them too deeply as this often leads to the formation of a higher root system. Firm the soil lightly but avoid excessive pressure. The idea is to provide a light, nutritious soil, through which roots can pass easily, thus leading to a corresponding development of strong branches and trunk.

Water the tree in well and then watch for shoot activity before resuming the Stage I watering schedule. As a rule of thumb, it is better to be a little on the dry side than over wet. If a period of heavy rain follows, it is worth rigging some plastic sheeting overhead to prevent water logging.

If all seems well and the tree grows strongly, feed with Phostrogen till the end of July. Change over to tomato type feed to season and ripen new growth both above and below the soil. Tomato feed is given monthly and make the last application, given any time in September, a mild one.

After the first month or so the tree should begin to grow strongly. In the first season the new growth may exceed 2 m (6 ft) in length. Do not prune these shoots. Protect from frost by rigging a poly-tent over the tree.

YEAR 2
In March when the buds break, trim back to about 2.5 cm (1 in) those shoots chosen for a leader and a couple of replacements. It is better to leave several until it becomes obvious that the ideal one is surviving. Trim other shoots close to the trunk but not flush. The aim is to build the trunk through the additional thickening provided by multi-shoot activity. By not trimming too closely, fresh bud activity starts up quickly, thus adding trunk weight through rapid expansion. Seal all cuts.

In the second season all the basal buds triggered by the Year 1 'trunk chop' and the Year 2 'shoot chop', are allowed full rein. Prune nothing.

Feed and water abundantly from

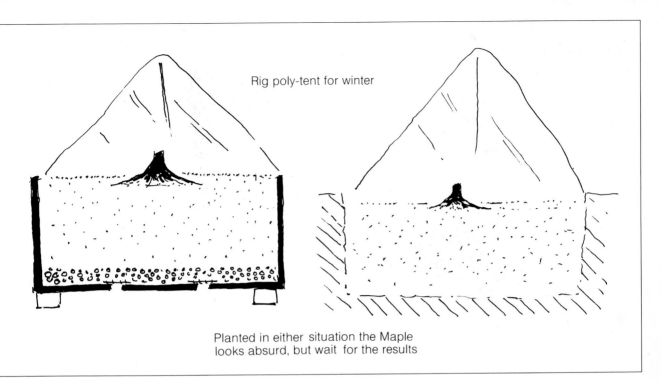

Rig poly-tent for winter

Planted in either situation the Maple
looks absurd, but wait for the results

YEAR 2
FAST TRUNK DEVELOPMENT
METHOD 1

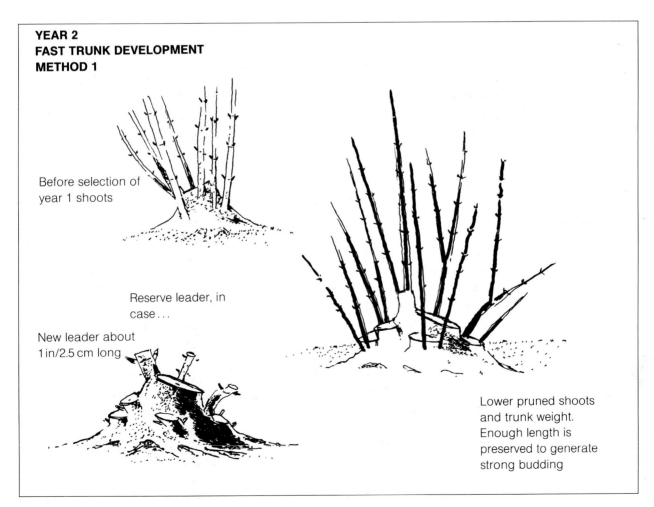

Before selection of
year 1 shoots

Reserve leader, in
case...

New leader about
1 in/2.5 cm long

Lower pruned shoots
and trunk weight.
Enough length is
preserved to generate
strong budding

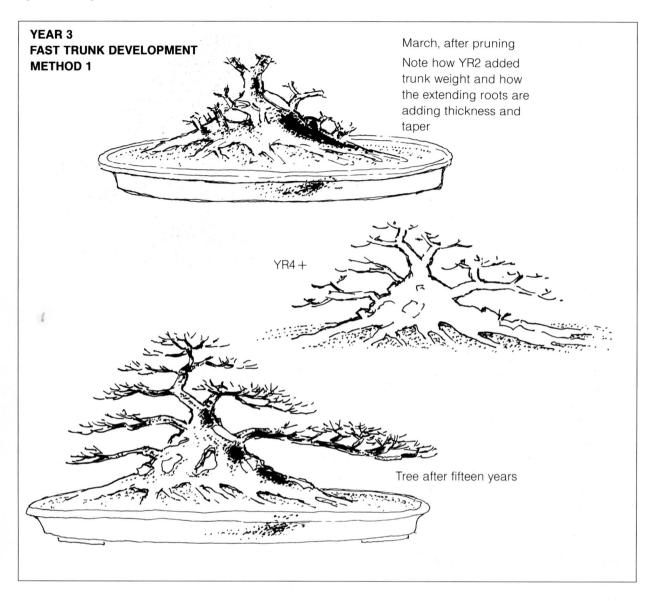

**YEAR 3
FAST TRUNK DEVELOPMENT
METHOD 1**

March, after pruning

Note how YR2 added trunk weight and how the extending roots are adding thickness and taper

YR4 +

Tree after fifteen years

March until July. Remember to harden the growth with tomato feed from the end of July to September.

Unlimited growth of roots and shoots initiates quite a basal flare to the trunk. The constant utilization of vigorous suckers body builds the lower trunk and the roots pull the line outwards as they fatten with the absorption of food and water.

Reduce shoot length to suit the winter poly-tent and seal all cuts.

YEAR 3

In March when the buds break, dig out the Maple and root prune to about a 30 cm (1 ft) circle round the trunk.

Trim shoots back, remembering to preserve enough at each base for compound budding. Seal cuts. Remember to retain a further 2.5 cm (1 in) on the chosen leader to preserve supremacy and taper.

Recycle as much of the soil as possible and make up with new. Add fresh peat, rotted manure and bone-meal and mix well. Replant the Maple and after the initial soaking, ease back the watering in the usual way. When the shoots are strong, water may be given according to the

An interesting alternative: an excellent clump with a massive base may be formed by retaining the shoots, in the most pleasing positions

usual schedule. Feed with Phostrogen till July then change over to tomato feed. Trim shoots to fit the winter poly tent and seal all cuts.

Repeat Year 2 and 3 cycles till sufficient girth and height are obtained. The principle of constant 'grow and chop' produces a squat, conical trunk of great power. The basal shoot production builds a solid base quickly. The heavy Trident Maple, tree no. 5, in the section on Structure and Form, was developed by this method.

Trunk scarring, if desired, may be featured instead of smoothed away. The scar tissue that is built up through the spur pruning may instead be hollowed in part and some knobs and warts left on for texture. The heavy Trident Maple mentioned above was hollowed out and looks very effective. See also the note under Trunk Scar Refinement.

FAST TRUNK DEVELOPMENT

METHOD 2

Appropriate for all Maples

Year 1
In March prepare a container or dig a hole as for Method 1.

In this technique the Maple is beheaded at a higher point above the root system. The cut is made at one third of the projected finished size, therefore select strongly grown material with a long trunk. Make the cut straight across the trunk and seal it immediately with wound seal. Try to cut in a well budded zone, but again, this is not too critical as many buds are triggered through pruning.

Trim and even the roots, then plant the tree at an angle of about 45°. Fill in with soil mixture but do not bury the tree too deeply. It may be necessary to remove some roots from the top of the new planting position if they cannot be teased down into the soil.

Water in well, then wait for further bud and shoot activity before restoring the Stage 1 water schedule. Remember the initial dryness helps the roots to settle. After a month if all seems well, water well and feed with Phostrogen, then change over to tomato feed. Do not prune shoots except to make them fit the poly-tent.

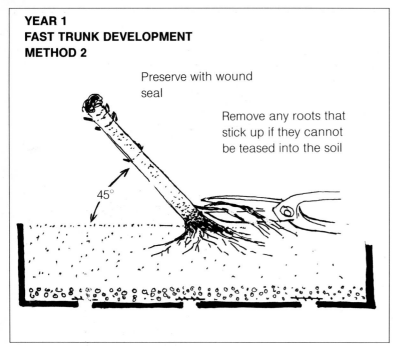

**YEAR 1
FAST TRUNK DEVELOPMENT
METHOD 2**

Preserve with wound seal

Remove any roots that stick up if they cannot be teased into the soil

45°

month, when the tree is stable once more, feed with Phostrogen to maximize the growth, but remember to change to tomato feed in July.

Soft pinch the side branch so a nucleus of growth is formed for training. The leader is pruned in August. Make the cut above a bud or shoot that points in a direction similar to the lower trunk line. Make the cut half the length of the first trunk division, that is, at a point that gives pleasant variation to the emerging line. Do not cut too closely to the bud in case of die-back. Preserve 2.5 cm (1 in) of shoot stub and seal the cut. The opposite bud will form the second branch. There is usually enough growing season left to help the new leader and second branch develop a little before dormancy. Place in the poly-tent over winter.

Repeat Year 2 and 3 cycles till the trunk thickens sufficiently. The tree is built on this repeat process of opposing angles. If less growing time is allowed between leader extensions towards the apex, the taper will be better and the space between each trunk pruning should shorten towards the apex.

Transplant the tree in Years 3, 5 and 7, and so on. The key is not to trim the roots too closely and to tip the shoots just enough to keep a balance. This enables the tree to benefit from the all important soil change without checking the development.

When the trunk is fat enough, the tree is root pruned to a circle of approximately 45 cm (1 ft 6 in) in diameter and is transferred to a shallower box to generate a more compact root system. In the next season the tree may be transplanted again into a bonsai pot, *if* the roots are densely packed. If they are not well formed, replace the tree and run on for another year.

YEAR 2

In March when the buds break, transplant the tree and trim back all shoots except the leader and first branch and two reserves in case those two should fail. If after a month the leader and first branch are strong, remove reserve shoots.

The leader is allowed free growth all the season. The side branch is pruned at the end of June. This avoids a power struggle where equally thick shoots rob the potential trunk line of maximum fattening. By pruning to avoid over thickening, the side branch is encouraged to put out side shoots that may also be developed. Seal the cuts.

Feed with Phostrogen until the end of July and then change to tomato feed. Water heavily if the summer rains are inadequate. Tip trim the leader and side branch to fit the poly-tent. Seal the cuts.

YEAR 3

In March when the buds break, the Maple is root pruned to a circle about 30 cm (1 ft) round the trunk. After a

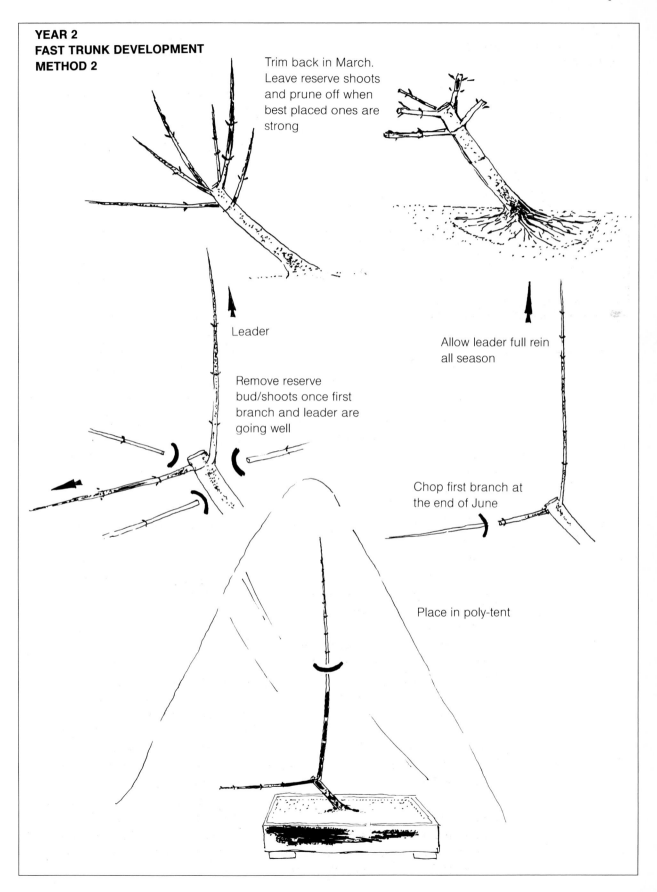

YEAR 2
FAST TRUNK DEVELOPMENT
METHOD 2

Trim back in March. Leave reserve shoots and prune off when best placed ones are strong

Leader

Remove reserve bud/shoots once first branch and leader are going well

Allow leader full rein all season

Chop first branch at the end of June

Place in poly-tent

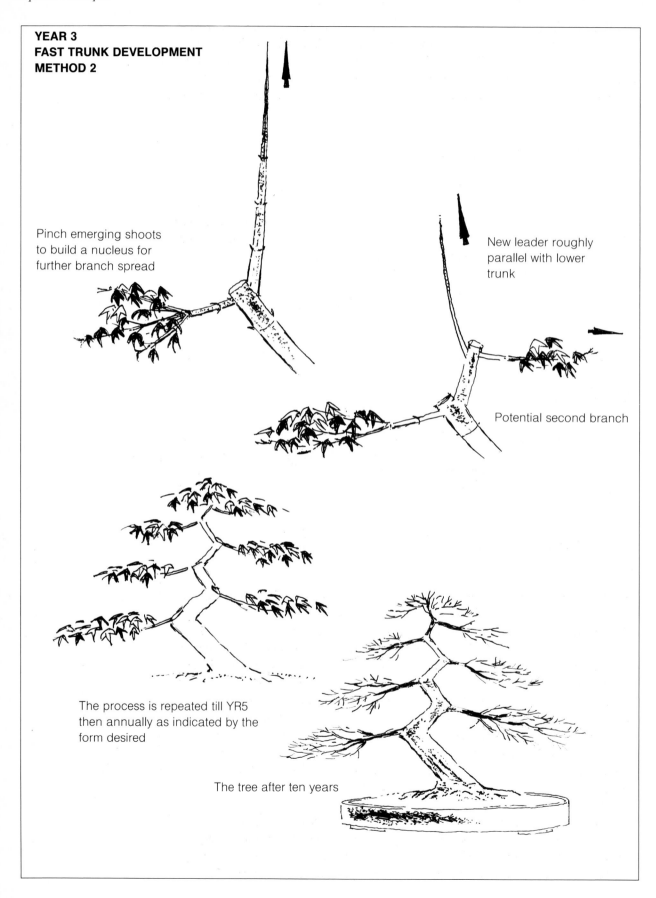

**YEAR 3
FAST TRUNK DEVELOPMENT
METHOD 2**

Pinch emerging shoots
to build a nucleus for
further branch spread

New leader roughly
parallel with lower
trunk

Potential second branch

The process is repeated till YR5
then annually as indicated by the
form desired

The tree after ten years

The idea behind this system is to produce a rapidly tapering tree with good visual movement. The idea of 'cut and grow' has fallen into disrepute recently since some Japanese exporters started sending incomplete examples, where a heavy base and tentative secondary stage trunk only are supplied. All such trees need extra time following the process shown.

LAYERING METHODS

SINGLE TREES

Appropriate for all Maples

This is the technique by which one can select a desirable section of a large tree, encourage it to root and then grow it as a new tree. The technique may be used in a chain of events such as in the raising of a root connected tree. Above all it is a way of utilizing redundant material rather than consigning it to the rubbish bin. The basic technique is simple to do and great fun.

The best season is in early spring as the leaves open.

LAYERING METHODS

ROOT CONNECTED GROUPS

Appropriate for all Maples

In this technique a group is formed by spreading out a clump Maple, layering it beneath the forked area, and encouraging shoot development from the prostrate limbs. These are then trained up as trees. The best season is in early spring.

GROUPS FROM SEEDLINGS AND CUTTINGS

Appropriate for all Maples

In this style of planting many trunks are assembled as the name suggests. One of the key aims of group bonsai is to create a mood and an image of a natural grove. Horticulturally, the method is simple, and merely requires the production of material of differing sizes, similar trunk form, varying complexity of branches, and identical growth characteristics. Thicks and thins, tall and short, all have their place.

Broadly speaking, an assembly that works well is when a heavy tree taken as the focal point, is placed at one third along the major axis of the container on the centre line and is then flanked by two or more trees of lesser size. A triangular formation is thus created. This is then echoed with another triangular formation of trees of lesser dimensions, allowing space between the two masses, which increases the perspective. As trees recede into implied distance they should become smaller and simpler, whereas foreground trees should be bigger and multi-branched. There is sound horticulture behind this, remembering that all trees but particularly Maples heavy up in general appearance when densely leaved and branched. So by keeping the lighter trees leaf-thinned and

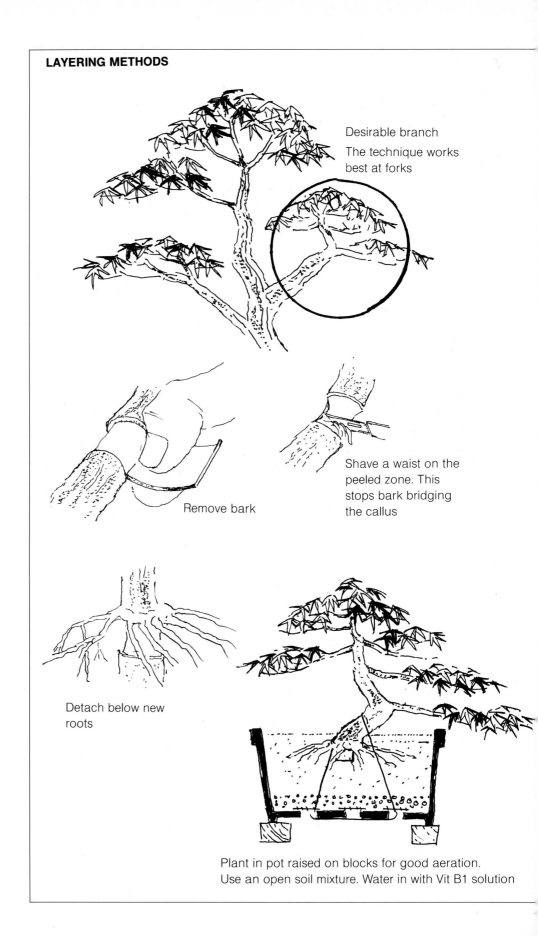

LAYERING METHODS

Desirable branch
The technique works best at forks

Remove bark

Shave a waist on the peeled zone. This stops bark bridging the callus

Detach below new roots

Plant in pot raised on blocks for good aeration.
Use an open soil mixture. Water in with Vit B1 solution

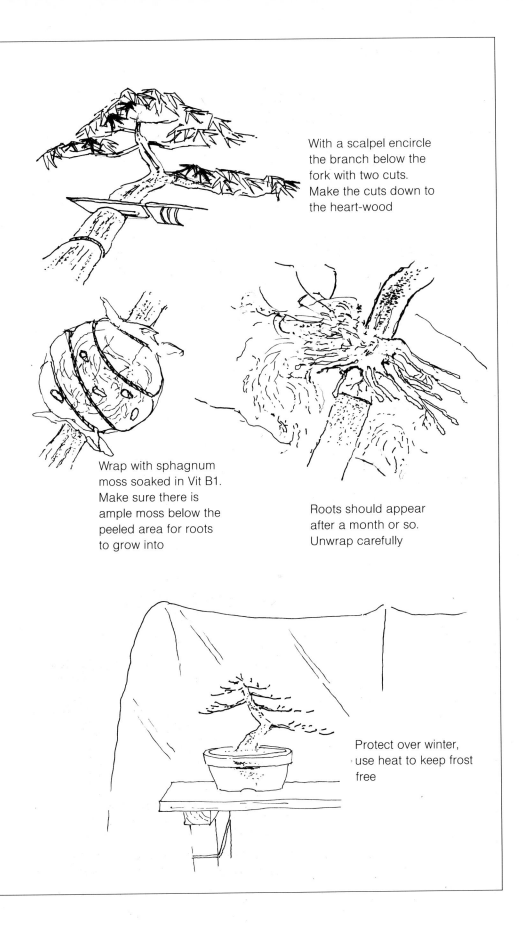

With a scalpel encircle
the branch below the
fork with two cuts.
Make the cuts down to
the heart-wood

Wrap with sphagnum
moss soaked in Vit B1.
Make sure there is
ample moss below the
peeled area for roots
to grow into

Roots should appear
after a month or so.
Unwrap carefully

Protect over winter,
use heat to keep frost
free

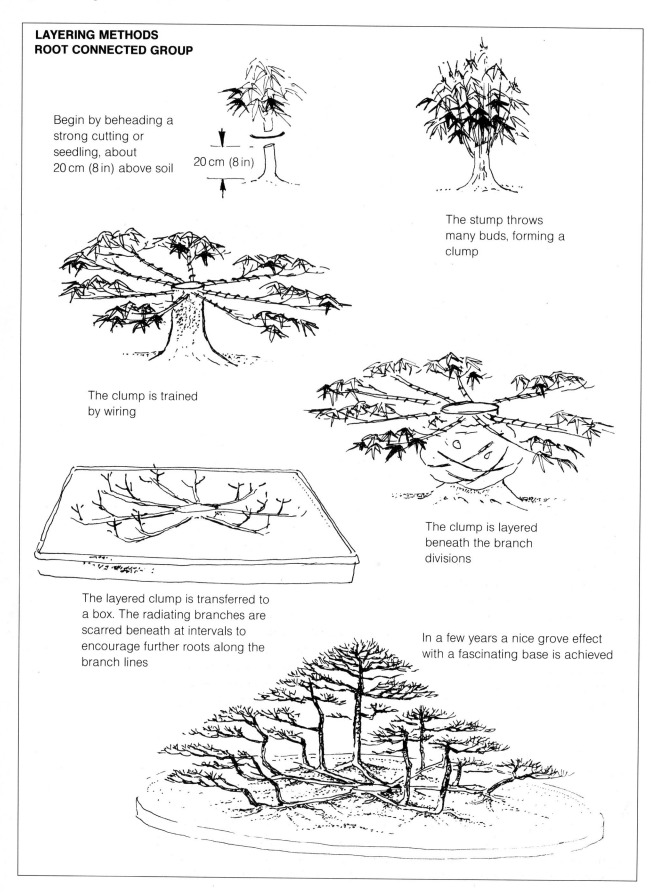

LAYERING METHODS
ROOT CONNECTED GROUP

Begin by beheading a strong cutting or seedling, about 20 cm (8 in) above soil

20 cm (8 in)

The stump throws many buds, forming a clump

The clump is trained by wiring

The clump is layered beneath the branch divisions

The layered clump is transferred to a box. The radiating branches are scarred beneath at intervals to encourage further roots along the branch lines

In a few years a nice grove effect with a fascinating base is achieved

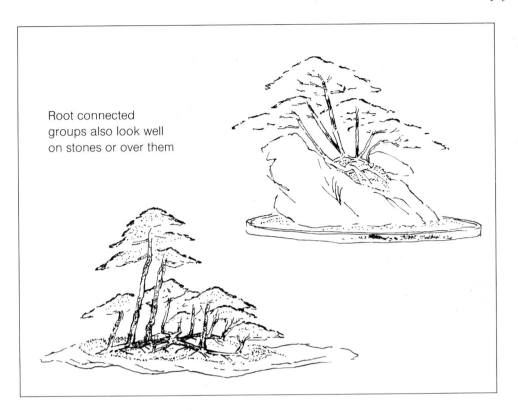

Root connected
groups also look well
on stones or over them

groomed, a pleasant relationship may be maintained.

Avoid masking trunk lines completely but otherwise there is vast scope for placement. The spaces between trunks are as important as the thicks and thins of the trunks. If more weight of trunk is needed, allow a line to pass slightly in front of another and the overlapping will appear to add weight. Make sure that the ground plan is irregular and avoid a rank and file appearance.

The horticultural process of creating material for groups is as suggested for raising Maples without trunk wiring, where natural looking trees result from the 'prune and grow' system. In the formation of a group, trees that resemble each other are used to make a harmonious arrangement.

Assemble the group by selecting trees that were grown in the same depth of soil, but in containers of different length and breadth. This will yield trees of differing heights and thicknesses. Choose carefully so that every tree relates to the chosen theme.

Prepare the container with tie-wires and a drainage course. Begin placement with the major tree. This should stand on a prominence, so mound the mix under the main trunk. The root systems will often have to be pruned as group placement proceeds so that trunks may butt together as required. Tie in the major tree with cross wires passing over the main roots, place the other smaller trees in their chosen positions on slightly less elevated mounds, and tie in. Site the main tree in the second nucleus diagonally back from the main group. Preserve a gap between, tie in, and place and tie the subordinate trees into position. Fill in with soil mix and contour the surface around the twin nucleii. Rounded forms usually look nice.

If trees are butted together they

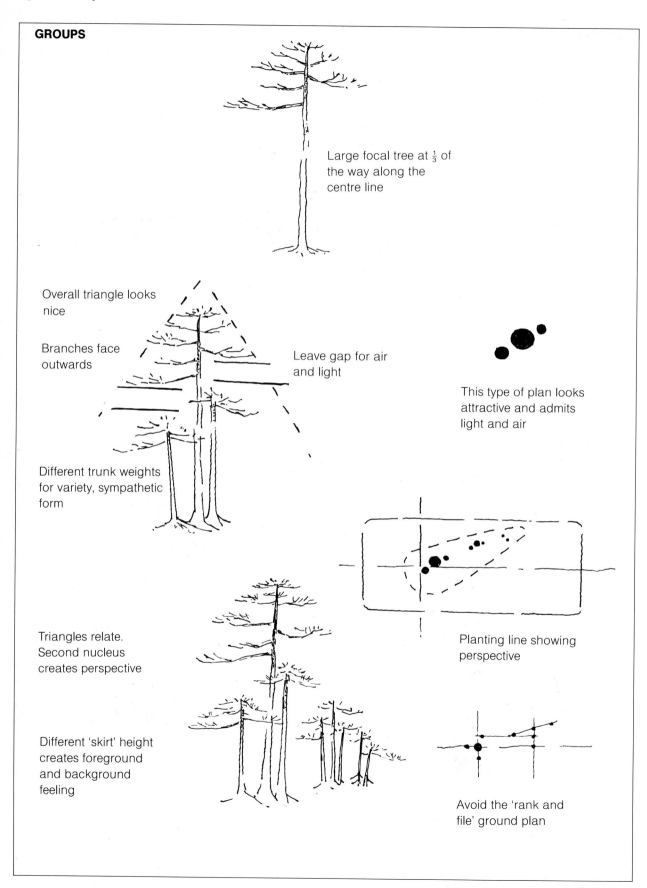

GROUPS

Large focal tree at ⅓ of the way along the centre line

Overall triangle looks nice

Branches face outwards

Leave gap for air and light

This type of plan looks attractive and admits light and air

Different trunk weights for variety, sympathetic form

Triangles relate. Second nucleus creates perspective

Planting line showing perspective

Different 'skirt' height creates foreground and background feeling

Avoid the 'rank and file' ground plan

GROUPS

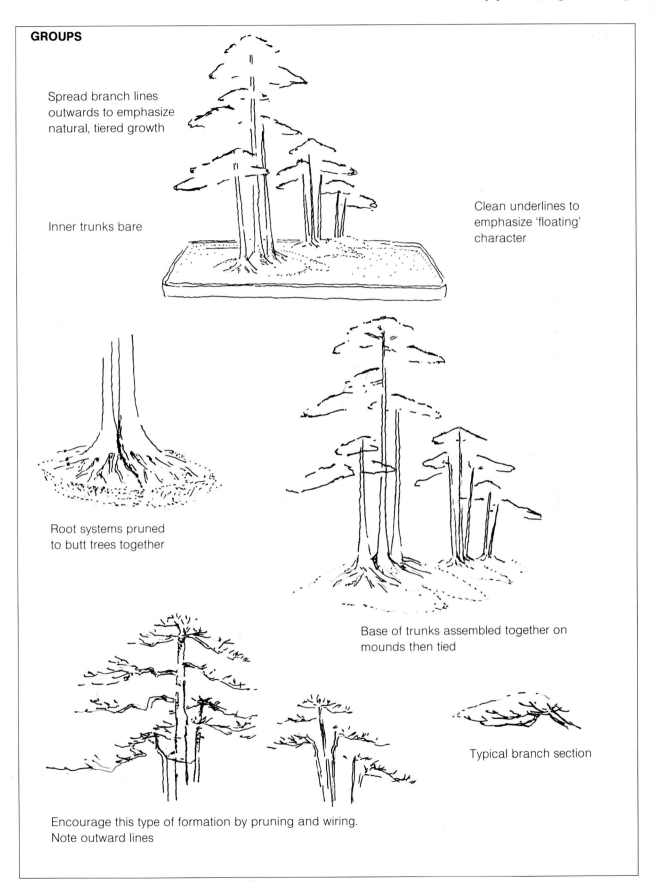

Spread branch lines outwards to emphasize natural, tiered growth

Inner trunks bare

Clean underlines to emphasize 'floating' character

Root systems pruned to butt trees together

Base of trunks assembled together on mounds then tied

Typical branch section

Encourage this type of formation by pruning and wiring. Note outward lines may be tied with string at the base of their trunks for extra stability. Root masses tied to each other also help stability. Water in well with Vitamin B1 solution and follow usual growing season schedules for Stage 1 and so on, as the group ages.

As the trees shoot, encourage tiered lines that are typical of the species, styling branches to flow outwards, achieving angular lines by pruning and soft bends by wiring. Protect newly assembled groups from high winds and other weather extremes for at least two seasons. They need to root together and form a pad. Check root ties are not constricting anything.

RAFT STYLE
Appropriate for all Maples

Neither a layering, nor group, but somewhere between the two, raft planting is formed by laying a tree on its side and inducing roots along the underside. The branches are trained to become 'trees'. When the induced root system is strong enough, the parent root system is often dispensed with or severely reduced. This lightens the appearance and encourages the roots now distributed along the trunk to thicken, and with

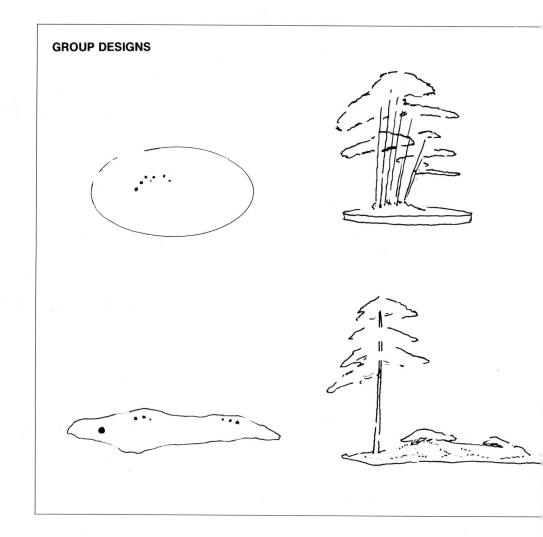

GROUP DESIGNS

time, to become a surface feature.

In the early spring as the leaves burst, the intended raft has all the underneath branches removed. Some side branches are retained. All upper branches are wired into position and the side branches where appropriate.

Flaps of bark are removed by scoring squares with a scalpel and then peeling the outer bark down to the sapwood. All these cuts are made on the underside. Paint the peeled areas with rooting hormone. That section of the root ball projecting upwards when the trunk is reclined, is removed or much reduced. The lower section of root mass is encouraged to flatten along beneath the trunk.

Prepare the container with a good drainage course and tie strings. The container need not be a bonsai tray—a box is quite good enough for this stage. Remember to raise the container for ventilation. Lay the tree down and tie into position. Encourage lower roots along the trunk line and smooth and blend the upper root line. The soil level should cover about half the trunk depth. Water in well with Vitamin B1 solution then hold the water till dryness is seen. There will be a lot of water standing around with insufficient root mass as yet to utilize it and one must monitor water carefully for a month or so. The after care for raft groups is as for other groups.

RAFT STYLE

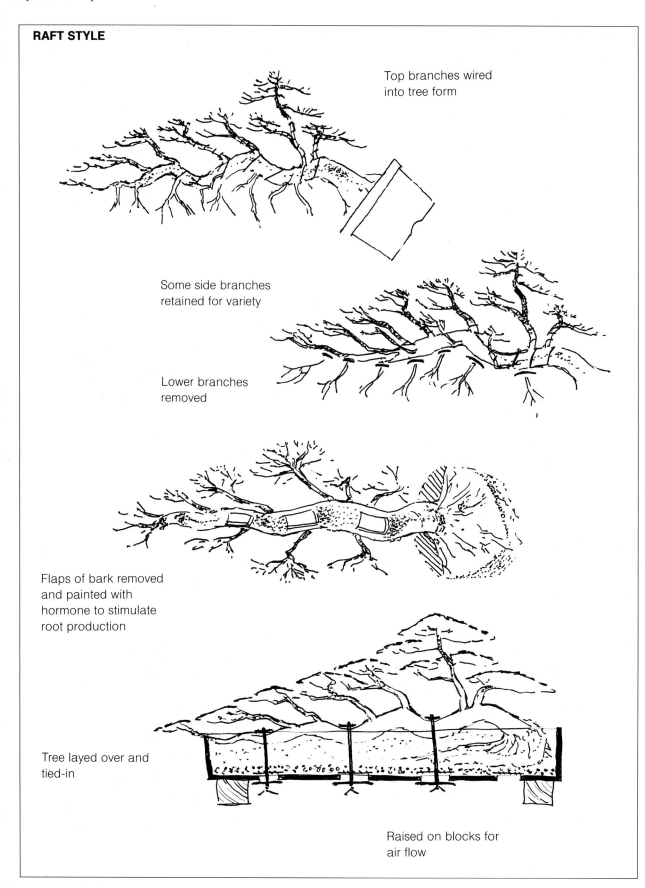

Top branches wired
into tree form

Some side branches
retained for variety

Lower branches
removed

Flaps of bark removed
and painted with
hormone to stimulate
root production

Tree layed over and
tied-in

Raised on blocks for
air flow

RAFT DESIGNS

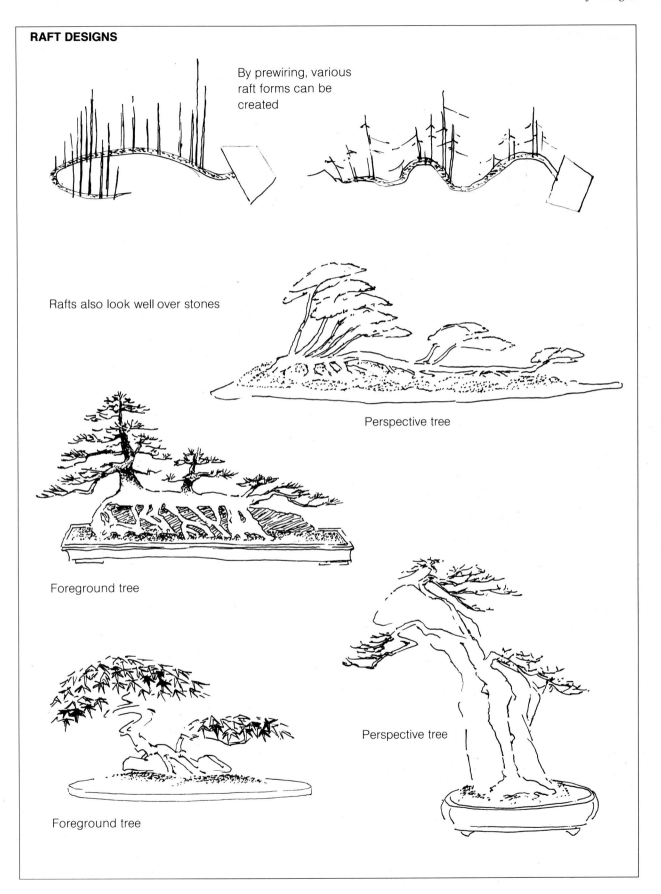

By prewiring, various raft forms can be created

Rafts also look well over stones

Perspective tree

Foreground tree

Foreground tree

Perspective tree

ROOT OVER STONE
Appropriate for all Maples

This technique as the name suggests, offers some of the most decorative possibilities for bonsai Maples. The concept derives from trees growing in the mountains and shows the eroded root system. Much fun can be had visualizing the sort of mood to be created: perhaps a gentle single tree over a low rounded stone, a group over stone, a raft or root connected tree over stone and so on.

The timing for this technique is again early spring. The method is to match tree and stone together first. Regardless of form, if large trees and small stones are used, the effect generated is that of a full grown tree.

If large stones and small trees are combined, enormous perspective is created.

First ensure that the stone is stable and if not, chisel or grind it flat. Mark the proposed planting area on the stone with a spirit marker pen. Wash the roots off, divide them gently into bunches and sit the tree in position and try arranging the roots down any fissures that the stone may offer. Ensure the roots are long enough to tuck beneath the stone. If all seems well, the next step is to remove the tree, wrapping the roots to keep them moist, and to prepare a planting paste of equal parts peat and

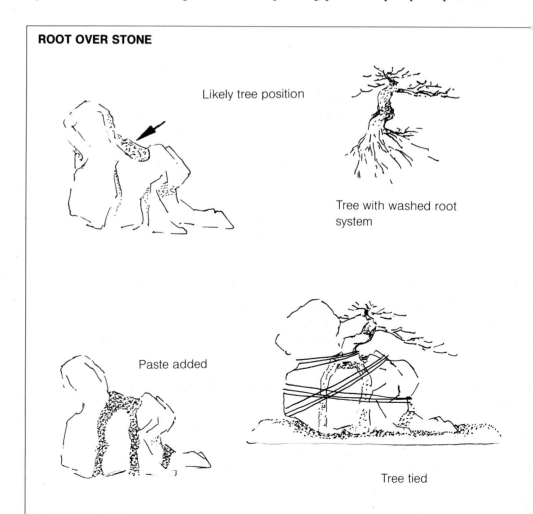

ROOT OVER STONE

Likely tree position

Tree with washed root system

Paste added

Tree tied

loam mixed well with water. Try not to make the paste too sloppy as it will have to 'stay' like cement.

Place an area of paste on the rock where the tree will sit and then down the roots' chosen path over the rock. Place the tree in position over the paste and wiggle it a little to settle it down. Tie the trunk into position with string. Arrange the roots into bunches and place them along the paste smeared fissures. My friend Dan Robinson in Seattle, USA discovered that if some finger pressure is applied to the roots to macerate them a little, then a flat, spreading coalition of the roots ensues at a very young age. Either way, add more paste over the roots and press a little fine moss over the top and tie the roots with more string. As a further reinforcement of Dan Robinsons's discovery, I have noticed that where the roots of Maples over stone imported from Japan have been heavily bound, they have flattened, and where left to their own devices have remained pencil like and not really gripped the stone. Dan's full technique after maceration is to encase the root mass in aluminium baking foil and to place earth over the top of the foil to keep everything in close register to the stone. This brilliantly innovative technique creates superb webbing of the roots without those awful wire marks.

Do not cover more of the stone surface with paste than is necessary, as this looks unsightly, but more

Roots tentatively placed

A root that reappears like this adds interest

The tree after ten years

USING LAYERED MATERIAL

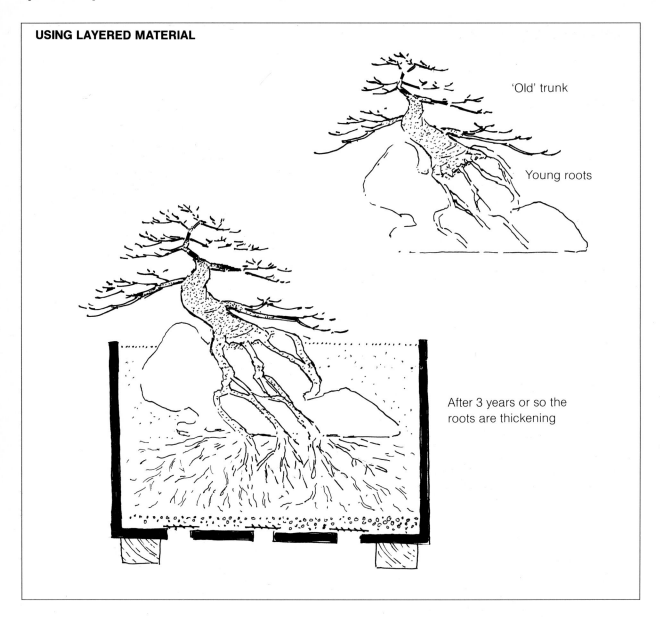

'Old' trunk

Young roots

After 3 years or so the roots are thickening

importantly, encourages root bunching rather than flatter roots that hold well. Finally, place the planting in a bonsai pot prepared with soil and tie-strings and tuck the root ends under the stone. Tie the stone down with the strings. This stabilizes the unit until the root pad is formed. Place in shade, water with Vitamin B1 solution and follow standard aftercare.

Another method with Root over Stone Maples that gives a beautiful result is to layer a tree, such as that grown by the Fast Trunk Develop-

ment methods, and then to attach this heavy trunk to the stone. The advantage of this system is twofold: the look of an old tree is instantly captured; and also the tree has a very young root system that readily hugs the stone.

To make the roots fatten rapidly and blend in appearance with the tree, the assembled unit is deep planted in a box with a good, well drained soil, and grown without disturbance for three to five years. To avoid root scarring with the ties,

ROOT OVER STONE DESIGNS

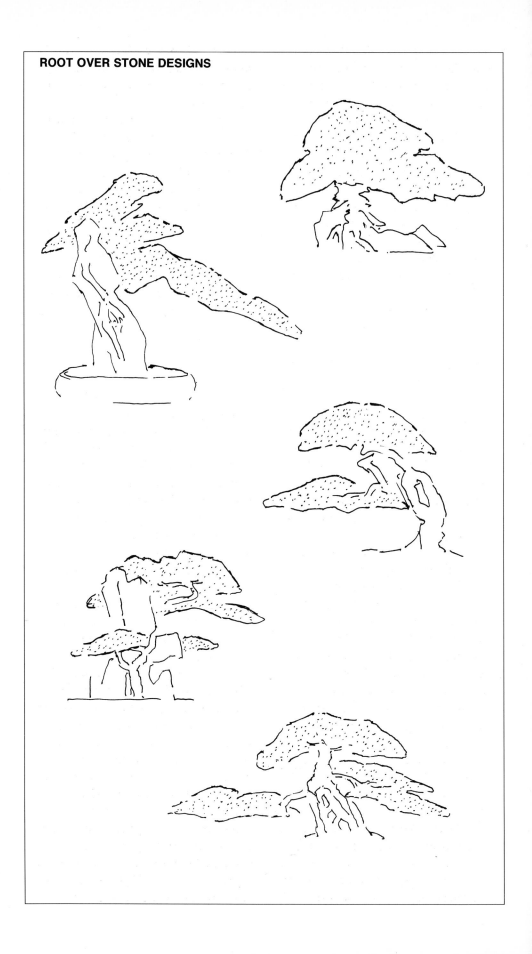

ROOT OVER STONE DESIGNS

use something like raffia that will rot. Provided time is taken when attaching the tree so that the roots hug the stone, the external soil pressure will hold them in position after the ties rot. Alternatively, after one year, it might be well worth considering using Dan's maceration technique and removing the tree from the box to add further paste and baking foil pressed in on to the root system before replanting.

At the end of the root development period the box is dismantled. There will be a mass of root fibre and enough is preserved to make a good pad around and below the base of the stone. The fuzz of fine hair roots up and down the decorative major root lines is removed.

Replant the tree-and-stone unit in a box about half the depth of the development container and tie in for stability. Add paste and press moss over the newly exposed roots to support them a little. The roots will reappear within the year as watering washes away the paste and moss. With exposure to the air, bark will start to form on the roots. Aftercare is standard, and you should repot into a bonsai container in another two years.

ROOT ATTACHED TO STONE
Appropriate for all Maples

A method that also gives a striking result is where the tree or trees are planted with their roots confined on the stone. Trident Maple and the *Yatsubusa* forms are very good for this, as their production of fine twigs offers the chance to detail and refine the design.

The technique usually generates more of a landscape effect than Root over Stone. Remarkably beautiful plantings can be created using the stone contour as a cliff or mountain, from which plants can either flow gracefully, or huddle against as low, dense forms. The rock or slab may also be very shallow and appear as a promontory or dish. There are of course countless variations between the two.

The method for attaching trees is as follows. For tall stones or rounded forms, surround the chosen planting spot with rings formed from aluminium or copper wires. These should be firmly glued to the stone. There is a new Japanese preparation that is very fast acting, consisting of cement and hardener, however, it is so fiddly that the job becomes a two-man undertaking. The ten second setting period somewhat offsets this difficulty, though sometimes a third person is needed to remove the two people from the stone! Otherwise, slower epoxy glues are fine. Tie strings securely to the loops and smear the planting area with the peat/loam paste mentioned in the previous section. Some people add extra clay, rotted cow manure and various additives to act as feed and reservoir for root support where hot weather is usual.

The tree is placed in the desired position with the roots trimmed to a reasonably compact state, horticulturally commensurate with the areas of branch spread and root circle. Do not remove so much that an imbalance is created between the two. Place the tree in the final position and check before tying securely. Do not use excessive pressure when securing the root system. It might be wise to use some cushioning material to avoid marking the roots. If the lower edge of the root ball swings under the

ROOT ATTACHED TO STONE

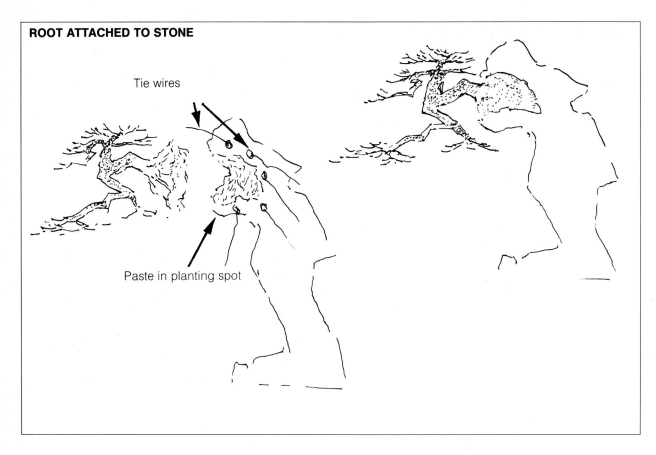

Tie wires

Paste in planting spot

ROOT ATTACHED TO STONE
SHALLOW STONE METHOD

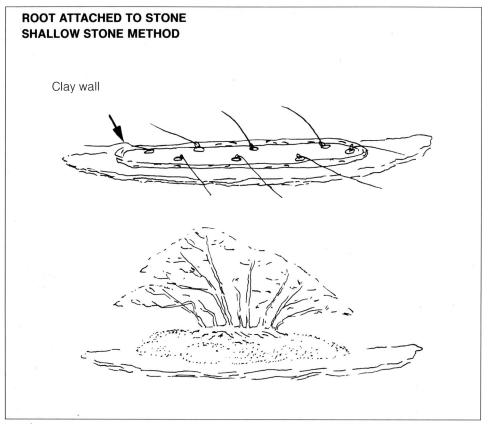

Clay wall

ROOT ATTACHED TO STONE DESIGNS

ROOT ATTACHED TO STONE DESIGNS

stone, it should be supported with fine plastic net to prevent erosion.

Add more paste and make sure it penetrates down between the roots. This is one of the situations where a chopstick is useful, but be cautious! The idea is to push the paste in, not to skewer the roots. Dress the surface with fine mosses and pin them into position with plastic covered wire staples. Spray the whole unit with a fine water jet and, after placing in shade, aftercare is standard.

With shallow or dishlike stones the method of planting is identical, except for the addition of a clay wall that surrounds the planting area to prevent erosion and to act as a reservoir.

TRUNK SCAR REFINEMENT
Appropriate for all Maples

In the process of fast trunk development, there will often be large areas of scar tissue on the lower trunk where trunk building branches have been removed. These stubs and swellings may be transformed into natural looking wounds by hollowing them out.

First, draw the desired form on the trunk with a spirit marker pen, then incise the line with a scalpel. Next use a chisel to chip out a narrow trench inside the scalpel cut, then the bark inside the line is removed. Chisels, jin pliers, and if necessary, electric tools are used to gouge out a natural looking depression, taking advantage of the textured look of the wood grain. This initial cut will be into wet wood which will 'feather'. I prefer to let the wood dry and rework it to remove this feathering.

It is as well to protect the surrounding area of the trunk before one begins. Wear eye protection and gloves. After operating, shade the tree and spray the exposed wood with a fungicide. The best season for this type of exercise is after the main growth is completed for the season, which is generally in late summer unless the weather is too hot. This gives the tree time to heal before winter and helps minimize potential frost damage. Freshly worked trees should be protected from frost.

Later, when the wood dries out, it may be preserved with lime sulphur which can be tinted to suit one's personal taste. Usually, decayed timber on deciduous trees appears brownish, so a little sepia or umber poster paint mixed with the lime sulphur will calm down the dead white appearance. Decayed timber is never unrelieved or even in tone, so when dry, try adding a little black poster paint to make the colour less even. The wood will 'naturalize' in appearance after a year or two.

FALSE BARK

In early spring one year I had the misfortune to encounter a bark munching beetle that had completely stripped the apical area of an old

Longhorn Beetle—*Anoplohora Chinensis*

THREAD GRAFTING

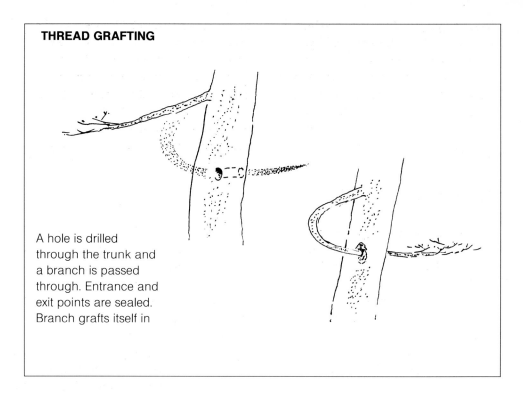

A hole is drilled
through the trunk and
a branch is passed
through. Entrance and
exit points are sealed.
Branch grafts itself in

ROOT GRAFTING

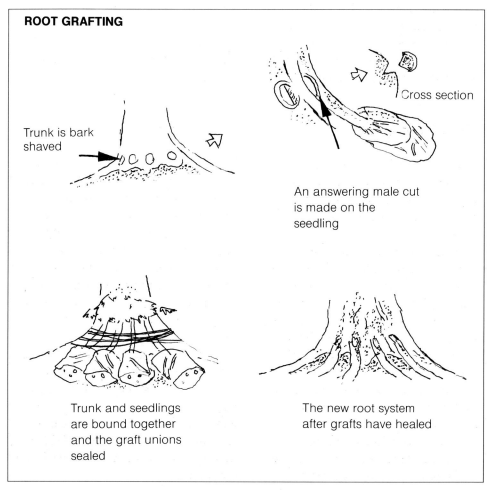

Trunk is bark
shaved

Cross section

An answering male cut
is made on the
seedling

Trunk and seedlings
are bound together
and the graft unions
sealed

The new root system
after grafts have healed

Trident Maple. The head was in full leaf on a skeletal frame! Luckily, I found the damage before any sap had dried and immediately applied liquid wound seal paint liberally all over the exposed heartwood. The tree was then moved into a shaded greenhouse with good ventilation and kept there for a week or two. The leaves wilted a little for a day or so then picked up. This is another proof that stabilization of the moisture content is the key to overcoming damage with these species. (See notes under Watering for the benefits related to moisture stabilization with damaged foliage.)

THREAD GRAFTING

This technique is one which enables the grower to programme the branches of a bonsai almost at will.

The best season for this type of grafting is in late spring to early summer. The technique consists of drilling through a shallow cord of trunk, finishing at the point where one would like the desired branch to emerge.

Use a sharp hand drill and take it slowly. Select a conveniently placed adjacent branch of the appropriate caliper, curve it down and thread it gently through the drilled hole. Each situation is slightly different. In some cases it is necessary to shape the branch with wire so it stays in position, and sometimes a light positioning tie will hold it in place. In all cases choose a branch that is long enough to complete the job. Seal the entry and exit points using wound seal paint to make the union airtight. The parent branch may be cut off when it becomes obvious that the new branch line has knitted with the trunk at the base. Usually it is best to wait for a season before trimming away the parent.

ROOT GRAFTING

The technique of root grafting employs the time-honoured 'approach graft method' and enables the grower to display ideally placed surface 'roots'.

Again, the best season is in late spring to early summer. Take well established, potted, two to three year old seedlings and with each one carve away two small sections of bark and heartwood, making the cuts back to back so a raised 'V' or male form results. Make the cuts at a point that will leave enough length of surface root when the seedlings are laid down flat. Each seedling trunk line will become a 'root' line in future.

Answering female 'V's' are carved in the base of the trunk zone that lacks root and the two prepared areas are united without delay. Make sure, of course, that the heads of the seedlings point towards the trunk. Make sure each union is securely bound. If they remain loose, try skewering them by tapping cocktail sticks through the recumbent seedlings to pinion them above and below the graft. Seal all graft areas with wound seal paint.

Allow a season before investigating the graft area. Successful grafts may be beheaded and the new root line may be unpotted and have its roots teased down into the soil. Be gentle so as not to upset the union. Trident Maples in particular respond well to root grafting.

SUMMARY CHART OF THE DEVELOPMENT OF JAPANESE MAPLE BONSAI

	YEAR 1	YEAR 2	YEAR 3
JANUARY	Seed stratified from Autumn	Winter protection. Keep damp.	
FEBRUARY	Seed stratified from Autumn.	Winter protection. Keep damp.	
MARCH	Plant seed/insert cuttings. Spray with Benomyl fortnightly. Greenhouse.	Winter protection. Give Vit B1 if growth is weak. Keep damp. Check bud activity. Water may need increasing.	Transplant dry. Then prune trunks. Seal them, then water in with Vit B1. Winter protection.
APRIL	Seedlings may be pricked out if growing strongly. Vit B1 weekly, Benomyl fortnightly. Greenhouse.	As for March. Give Vit B1 fortnightly. Trim if necessary.	Winter protection. Feed 4 weeks after root disturbance. Feed schedule Stage I, $\frac{1}{2}$ strength. Vit B1 if weak.
MAY	Weekly Benomyl. 4 weeks after root disturbance, *weak* feed or Phostrogen. Place outside, watch frost. Spray for pests.	Place on benches in shaded Greenhouse. Feed/water schedules Stage 1, $\frac{1}{2}$ strength. Spray pests, $\frac{1}{2}$ strength.	As for YR 2. Feed schedule for Stage II. Full for vigorous plants.
JUNE	Strongly upright side shoots are shortened. Feed Phostragen every 10 days. Spray for pests.	As for May. Change feed over to 0–10–10-tomato feed	
JULY	As for June.	As for June.	
AUGUST	Shorten any lower shoots of strong. Check and retrim to reinforce cone. If necessary.	As for June. Give final pruning.	
SEPTEMBER	Keep damp.		
OCTOBER	Place in Greenhouse after first frosts. Remove all fallen leaves. Clean off all persistant leaves. Spray Benomyl.		
NOVEMBER	Winter protection. Keep damp.		
DECEMBER	Winter protection. Keep damp.		
	Note: Between March and September, water is given to keep evenly damp. Do not keep soggy.		

	STAGE II STRUCTURE AND FORM	STAGE III REFINEMENT OF IMAGE
YEAR 4	**YEAR 5**	**YEAR 6**

'Paint Prune'

As for YR 2. Increase water once shoots are seen. Feed schedule for Stage I for vigorous plants. Vit B1, for weak ones. Winter protection.	Increase water as buds open. Follow Water and Feed Schedules for Stage II. Place on shelf in Greenhouse. Winter protection. Dewire.	Root prune dry. Transplant to bonsai pot if trunks are heavy enough. Prune branches, seal cuts. Water in with Vit B1. Winter protection.
As for March.	As for March.	Winter protection. Feed 4 weeks after root disturbance. Restore water when growth is sound. Feed and Water schedule for Stage III.
Feed/water schedules for Stage I. Spray for pests. Place outside. Pinch growth to maintain cone.	Feed/water schedules for Stage II. Spray for pests. Place outside. Pinch growth to maintain cone.	Apart from new Feed/Water Schedules Stage III—follow YR 5.
Feed/water schedules for Stage I. Spray for pests. Prime paint coded branches. Seal cuts. White trunks and branches.	As for May. Heavy branches pruned if necessary. Train twigs into replacement position.	
As for June.	As for June.	

STAGE I DEVELOPMENT OF MASS

TREE NO. 1
Trident Maple Group Style

Offering picture 1981. Trident Maple group 63 cm (25 in) high, 40(!) years. Pot, dark green unglazed oval 54 × 36 × 4 cm (21 in × 14 in × 1½ in)

1. ROOT ESTABLISHMENT

The group was imported in the winter of 1981/82 and was planted in a larger pot than that supplied, to give additional root run. The planting soon became solidly settled and grew strongly in the first season. The chosen container was a dark green, unglazed oval, measuring 54 × 36 × 4 cm (21 × 14 × 1½ in). It acted as a good reservoir—always important with Trident Maple—and as an aesthetic underpinning to the projected, extending branch lines. The group was repotted in spring 1987 using a buff, glazed oval measuring 59 × 38 × 6.5 cm (23 × 15 × 2½ in). The branch lines needed counterweight to balance the design and there is even more root mass to keep happy.

2. TRUNK DEVELOPMENT

The 'imported age' was quoted as being 40 years. I estimate around 10 years as being nearer the mark.

The group would have been started from cuttings or seedlings assembled in a nuclear arrangement not unlike a 'comma' form when viewed from overhead. Thicks and thins were selected in a variety of different heights. The planting was the usual one where the lesser specimens cluster around the taller, heavier trunks.

Each season the branches were arranged with wires and pinched out to keep growth within bounds. The Trident Maple is vigorous however, and, as the top growth was not checked adequately, the trunks became a little apically dominant. The group had been well fed and watered and this, combined with the over-gentle top pruning, had produced this result.

When I acquired the group, my job was to maintain the thicks and thins distributed throughout the arrangement, which was still handsome, and to enhance the proportions.

There are twenty-five trunks and to preserve the differences in thickness and height, and to keep the design evolving, I chose to feed using the schedule for Stage 1, and to monitor the leaf load on each trunk, bearing in mind that the wood fattens according to the burden it carries. So far, even with a further increase in

	1982	1983	1984	1985	1986	1987
ROOT ESTABLISHMENT	Potted into larger pot in spring		Repotted in spring			Repotted into larger pot in spring
TRUNK DEVELOPMENT	UNDISTURBED Foliage trimmed each year to maintain proportions.					
BRANCH TRAINING	Each year the emerging lines were trained sideways and then were spur-pruned each Autumn. The apical areas were kept light.					
ROOT DEVELOPMENT	Potted on having arranged roots	Undisturbed to build pad of roots	Repotted and combed out	Undisburbed to build pad of roots		Repotted and combed out
CHANGE OF POT	Dark green unglazed oval 21″ × 14″ × 1½″ 54 × 36 × 4 cm					Buff glazed oval 23″ × 15″ × 2½″ 59 × 38 × 6.5 cm

pot size in spring 1987, the proportions have remained constant.

3. BRANCH TRAINING
The method followed was to suppress the overly-emphatic top growth, and to redirect the vigour downwards by hard pruning, thus ultimately reversing the lollipop appearance of top heavy growth on fragile trunks.

Towards the end of the Japanese cycle all the branches had been allowed to sweep up. So, as I wanted a tiered group, you will see from the 1982 photo sequence (page 68) that the branches were trained flat. I used loose wires to coax the line without the vigorous extension caused by tight bending.

In successive seasons, the chosen spring shoots were wire curved (using plastic covered wire to insulate the soft tissue against metal contact) when they had made three to four pairs of leaves and were therefore strong enough to accept shaping.

4. ROOT DEVELOPMENT
The roots were already well meshed when the group came into the UK and were trimmed in 1984 and 1987.

A more searching repotting is scheduled for 1988 as I want to enhance the surface roots. This will necessitate the removal of finer roots to feature the main surface lines.

5. FUTURE EVOLUTION
I see this group as remaining essentially light and airy, and therefore, in future years, it will be important to maintain the tiered branching.

As the trees evolve, the next stage of structuring may well involve the removal of branches to strengthen the assymetrical appearance. The whole dynamic could alter through angular changes brought about with wiring, or deep pruning; or by the removal of lower branches to lift the foliage canopy; or by taking away lower branches at one end only so that the weight appears to shift sideways, away from the pruned area.

As the group stands, it is a pleasant arrangement evoking the feeling of natural woodland and as this sort of image is easy to make and gives real satisfaction, I am sure could be applied to most broad-leaved trees.

OPPOSITE:
Winter 1986. The
branch lines look
strong.

Summer 1985. Notice
the differences that
branch arrangement
has made in four
seasons (see page 68).

The mass before tiering the branches, 1982

Branches are wired, lowered and tiered

General view contrasting the unfinished portion

The mass opened up

Close up of trunks with lower branches removed

Finished tree, note the pile of branches!

STAGE I DEVELOPMENT OF MASS

TREE NO. 2
Mountain Maple Group Style

Offering picture 1981. Mountain Maple group 55 cm
(22 in) high, 30 years. Pot, dark brown unglazed oval
54 cm × 38 cm × 5 cm (21 in × 15 in × 2 in)

1. ROOT ESTABLISHMENT

The tree was imported in the winter of 1981 and was planted in the dark brown, unglazed oval pot supplied with the tree. The roots were well knitted together, with a light sandy soil mixture around the outer area and some heavier material internally. The pot appeared to drain well, but, unfortunately, there was little water run-off due to the flat base sitting squarely on the bench. This led to a lot of blackening at the bottom of the root mass caused by the excess water trapped in the floor of the pot. The root condition was discovered in spring 1983, when a change of pot had been decided. I cleaned the blackened areas away and found good white roots throughout the middle to upper zones where air was able to pass through easily. I dunked the pruned root mass in a bath of Vitamin B1 solution and potted it into the new container the next day. I placed the tree in a well ventilated greenhouse and it sprouted and grew happily after a week or two.

2. TRUNK DEVELOPMENT

The trunks were well formed in general with nice mature bark appearing, but some were a little heavy at the top where they had been pruned back to achieve different height differences. Where heavy wood is cut like this and the resulting sprouts are cropped back without thinning, it is often encouraged to produce coarse growth. To induce a better taper, several tops were removed during 1983/84 and side branches were restarted in their place, to minimize the clubbed appearance.

The balance of thicks and thins throughout the arrangement was pleasing and I monitored their progress, as with the Trident Maple group, by selective leaf thinning to ensure the even development of the trunks.

3. BRANCH TRAINING

The branches were generally pleasing but too dense, and were tending to rise and leave their previously wired positions. The density was caused by the mechanical cropping of terminal growth. When the shoots were reduced in number, trimmed and wired flat, the lines of the branches were clarified.

OPPOSITE:
Autumn 1983. A
projected change by
rotating the group 20°
clockwise, a tighter
trunk arrangement
results

Autumn 1983

Summer 1985
The present front

	1982	1983	1984	1985	1986	1987
ROOT ESTABLISHMENT	Potted in pot supplied	Repotted in spring	⟶	Repotted in spring	⟶	
TRUNK DEVELOPMENT	UNDISTURBED ⟶					
	Foliage thinned each year to maintain proportions.					
BRANCH TRAINING	Each year the shoots were thinned out, wired and large leaves were pinched off. Inner growths were removed.				⟶	
ROOT DEVELOPMENT	Initial placement	Repotted in spring Damaged root area removed	⟶	Repotted in spring Roots combed out	⟶	
CHANGE OF POT	Dark Brown unglazed oval 21″ × 15″ × 2″ 54 × 38 × 5 cm	Grey Buff unglazed oval 22″ × 14″ × 2″ 55 × 36 × 5 cm	⟶			

I decided to extend the side branches at each end of the planting and allowed the lower branches to extend vigorously. They were pruned back by mid-season to avoid fattening their parent trunks unduly. One of the difficulties in developing a group is how to control the thickness of outer trunks. As these have open root run and access to light and air they can easily become so heavy that they rival the taller, heavy trunks, often spoiling the perspective and sense of scale.

I trimmed the inner growths away from the branches to create spaces around the trunks and to emphasize the future outward flow of the foliage lines. In early to mid-season, to simplify the foliage mass, I reduced back to two pairs of leaves in the upper tree areas and allowed three pairs of leaves in the lower parts. Larger leaves were removed when they became oversized throughout the season, and all hanging foliage was trimmed away.

4. ROOT DEVELOPMENT

The roots were very well meshed when the group arrived in England. After the root cleansing operation in 1983, the group was placed higher in the new container and in order to lose the container-shaped root periphery, the outer zones were combed down to create the natural slope seen in the picture taken in summer 1985.

The surface roots are already well formed and will continue to thicken, becoming a pleasant feature of this group.

5. FUTURE EVOLUTION

If the group is extended by about 25 per cent of the mass, and the inner lines are kept open, so that the foliage is seen tiered on what is an already interesting structure of trunks and branches, I think a strong, and very 'Maple-like' grove design will result.

The pot chosen in 1983 was made by Gordon Duffett and is a 55 cm (22 in) oval in unglazed, grey/buff clay.

TREE NO. 3

Trident Maple, Twin Trunk, Root over Stone Style

Spring 1983

1. ROOT ESTABLISHMENT

The tree was started as a cutting in 1968 and was set over a stone in 1976. To gain enough root length, even though the stone was small, I first grew the tree in a deepish container for a couple of seasons. I wanted to make the image of a tree beside water with its roots exposed and so chose a small stone appropriate to the setting.

The tree was root washed and set astride the stone to test for placement. I decided to position the tree on the edge of the stone so the future line would flow from the root flare at the left, up through and to the right, along the right low branch, thereby increasing the sensation of overhanging imaginary water.

The standard technique for 'root over stone' was followed and the planting was made to fit a shallow oval pot, 54 cm (21 in) long. The tree took well and was repotted in 1980 and 1984, when the present container was chosen.

2. TRUNK DEVELOPMENT

The trunks were grown as simple thick and thin limbs for some years before definite decisions about height and width were made. I kept the minor trunk slender by foliage thinning. The height of the trunks were determined in 1980. Until that time the heads of both trees had been allowed to grow in a diffuse manner. In the summer of 1980, a friend of mine, Dave Claridge of Bristol, was helping me style various trees, and on this tree he flattened the branch system of both trunks, and so I decided to maintain his concept of the spreading tier rather than the previous rounded form. This dictated hard pruning on both trunks. On the major trunk, I reduced all conflicting multi-leaders and encouraged extra height in the one chosen limb throughout the season. I removed a large vertical trunk area on the minor trunk, so that the line flowed abruptly sideways. The abruptness I softened with wiring which resulted in a curve rather than a right-angle. In subsequent seasons leaf thinning preserved the balance between trunks.

3. BRANCH TRAINING

This was not seriously thought about

Summer 1985.
Trident Maple 54 cm
(21 in) high. Pot,
blue/grey glazed
rectangle
45 cm × 33 cm × 6.5 cm
(18 in × 13 in × 2.5 in).
20 years

	1968 ➤ **1976**		**1977**	**1978**	**1979**	**1980**
ROOT ESTABLISHMENT	Grown in training pot	Set over stone in spring				Repotted in spring
TRUNK DEVELOPMENT	Proportions maintained by leaf thinning					Trunks pruned in summer
BRANCH TRAINING	'Approximate' branch pads pinched to maintain' portions					Styled in summer
ROOT DEVELOPMENT	In 1974 pot was used to give root length	Set over stone	Encouraged to make a firm pad base by good feeding and watering schedules			Pad trim
CHANGE OF POT		Off white oval pot glazed 21″ × 15″ × 1½″ 54 × 38 × 4 cm				

74

Close-up of root detail

1981	1982	1983	1984	1985	1986	1987

Repotted
in
spring

Flattened tiering maintained with wiring and trimming

Pad
trim

Blue grey
rectangle
glazed
$18'' \times 13'' \times 2\frac{1}{2}''$
$46 \times 33 \times 6.5$ cm

until the tree was solidly established over the stone. Dave really set the theme and I have embellished it every year since 1980. The technique he used was that of wiring the branches outwards in rippling curves, using a flat overall profile. When I trained the new leader, I utilized the adjacent parallel shoots to create a three-dimensional fan so that an apical cone was formed. Branch lengths were pruned to achieve a broadly triangular form in the major trunk, and a flattened spreading form in the secondary trunk. Each growing season I followed the shoot and side leaf removal technique accompanied by the removal of any large foliage. This yielded many shoots and masses of small leaves.

4. ROOT DEVELOPMENT

The root system proper is dense and healthy, whilst that area clasping the stone is broadening each year. The base roots are beginning to flatten against the stone and to coalesce nicely.

As the area that grips the stone is small and the roots were already strong, I did not use Dan Robinson's pressure technique to flatten them. Had there been greater root expanse I certainly would have used it as I wanted the element of simple wooden knuckles gripping the stone.

5. FUTURE EVOLUTION

I see the main trunk remaining a tiered triangle, and the right hand trunk extending, if anything. Great fun can be had in thinning leaves as the twigs develop, so the ageing framework is seen clearly. Twigs and small branches can often be removed to show interesting inner structures.

The pot is glazed blue-grey rectangle measuring $46 \times 33 \times 6.5$ cm $18 \times 13 \times 2.5$ in). It provides a pleasant colour contrast with the tree throughout the season.

TREE NO. 4

Trident Maple Root over Stone Style

Front view. Spring 1983

1. ROOT ESTABLISHMENT

The tree was imported in the winter of 1981 and was planted in a deep training pot. The roots were reasonably well knitted together and a fairly good pad of fine root was clustered round the stone. After a month or two the whole unit felt solid in the pot and a change to a shallower container was planned for 1983, when a rectangular pot was chosen. This is the container shown in the spring 1983 photograph and it measures 45 × 33 × 7.5 cm (18 × 13 × 3 in) and was made by Gordon Duffett. The present oval pot was used in 1986.

2. TRUNK DEVELOPMENT

To enhance the trunk line several masking branches were removed in the summers of 1982, 1983 and 1984. This has had the effect of slowing trunk expansion, although there is some evidence of bark cracking which is an indication of thickening.

An apex was chosen in the summer of 1982 as an height reference only (I personally do not care for apexes as little trees) and then laterals were allowed to rise to round off the apex.

Back view.
Spring 1983

Root detail

Summer 1986. Trident
Maple, 60 cm (24 in) high.
Trunk diameter, 10 cm (4 in).
Pot, off-white glazed oval,
54 cm × 35 cm × 6.9 cm
(21 in × 14 in × 2¾ in).
Made by Gordon Duffett

OPPOSITE:
Winter 86/87. New front

	1982	1983	1984	1985	1986	1987
ROOT ESTABLISHMENT	Planted in temporary container	Repotted in spring			Repotted in spring	
TRUNK DEVELOPMENT	Minimal increase					
BRANCH TRAINING	Heavy branches removed in summer				Major restyle in summer	
	Branches built up by wiring extending growth, trimming, and thinning.					
ROOT DEVELOPMENT	Minimal main root thickening					
	Extra surface roots planned and now appearing					
CHANGE OF POT		Off white glazed rectangle 18″ × 13″ × 3″ 45 × 33 × 7.5 cm			Off white glazed oval 21″ × 14″ × 2¾″ 54 × 35 × 6.9 cm	

The taper on the trunk with the new apex positioned was impressive—seen from the back! Compare the front and back views in spring 1983.

3. BRANCH TRAINING

This consisted of the selective removal of over-dense and trunk-masking limbs, and the extending of other lines, using wiring, trimming and thinning techniques. The heavy branches were taken off at the same time each season—around June or July. The cuts were sealed to maintain moisture, thus keeping bud production unimpaired. Remember not to prune too closely if buds are required, as once the branch bases are removed, bud apparition becomes more random.

As the lines of the tree extended, a long low branch seemed the natural way to develop the right-hand side (see the picture taken in summer 1986). However, the reverse view, once extraneous branches were removed, offered tremendous rhythm and vitality through trunk and branches. I therefore chose the 'front' shown in the winter 1986 picture and removed several major branches in order to achieve the image shown in the drawing of the future form.

4. ROOT DEVELOPMENT

The root system is compact and healthy, and those clasping the stone really 'grip' when seen from the new front. I plan to bring a few more to the surface adjacent to the stone.

5. FUTURE EVOLUTION

The sum total of roots, stone angle, trunk dynamic and branch swing, have for me, much greater appeal from the new front. I plan to replant the tree to sit better in the pot in 1988. A lot of scope for enjoyment remains in the development of the low branch and the rising limbs that comprise its canopy, and the balancing of that against the abbreviated branch tiering of the upper trunk, to make a compelling winter silhouette.

TREE NO. 5
Trident Maple Twin Trunk Style

Trunk detail

1. ROOT ESTABLISHMENT

The tree was imported in 1981 by air shipment. I opened the crate and there was this wee hedgehog! About 46 cm (18 in) high and 25 cm (10 in) thick, tapering to nothing, it was one of five trees with amazing trunks and all were 15 years old! To get a true age was interesting, as normally, an advanced age is given to satisfy the Western fascination with 'ancient and tiny'. The tree had to be tied when potted as the root system was very loose. It grew strongly and in a month was already firming up in the pot.

2. TRUNK DEVELOPMENT

The trunk is a perfect example of the technique described under Fast Trunk Development Method 1, where basal shoots are utilized to build trunk weight.

By studying the trunk I have been able to analyse the probable sequence of steps in the development of this specimen. I estimate that around 1966, the tree was started from either a cutting or a seedling, developed first in a pot to establish it for a couple of seasons, before being transferred to open growth in a field. During field growth the tree was fed heavily using animal manure (which I could still smell when I imported it!) to boost heavy trunk expansion.

The trunk was probably chopped in the fourth year between spring and mid-season, to encourage base suckers.

I suspect transplanting was done at approximately five year intervals or something similar, in order to thicken the trunk really fast. Trees grow more vigorously if not disturbed too often. From the size of the scars where old material was removed, it is possible to project that the suckers were allowed some 3–6 m (10–20 ft) of vertical growth before removal, and thus assumed 2.5–7.5 cm (1–3 in) of thickness, thereby building base thickness by that amount in every case.

The main trunk appears to have been chopped at the same time and there are two distinct taper zones where the trunk was regrown after the leader was sacrificed. Both trunk and suckers would have been chopped at each five year transplanting.

Summer 1985. Trident
Maple 51 cm (20 in) high,
25 cm (10 in) diameter,
branch spread 81 cm
(32 in). 19 years. Pot,
blue glazed oval
56 cm × 33 cm × 5 cm
(22 in × 13 in × 2 in),
made by Gordon Duffett

Close-up of minor
trunk

Winter 1986/87. Pot, cream glazed oval 61 cm × 41 cm × 8 cm (24 in × 16 in × 3½ in), made by Gordon Duffett

At the age of ten years, or thereabouts, the minor trunk was approach grafted on to the main trunk. It was probably allowed 2–3 seasons to knit before being branched styled.

The main trunk is actually hollow and probably became so after sucker scars were allowed to rot unsealed. The effect is attractive and the health of the tree is unimpaired. The scooping out was assisted when the Longhorn Beetle incident (described in the False Bark note) culminated with his/her (let's not get chauvinistic here!) exit from the trunk. I have included a mug shot of this very Longhorn Beetle, *Anoplophora Chinensis*, and entomologists will no doubt note the sated smile!

3. BRANCH TRAINING
This was started seriously at around 10–11 years of age. The branches were allowed full rein after being wire shaped for the first 5–7.5 cm (2–3 in) or so. They would then have been chopped back in later summer, dewired and allowed to form strong side shoots. In autumn the side shoots would have been spur pruned. In the next season the side shoots would have been flattened to the branch plane by wiring and further trimming. In addition, every year, the foliage density would have been increased by the shoot and side/leaf removal technique, and then the whole system would have been repeated up to year 15.

After I purchased the tree I continued each process, after first removing overgrown and crowded branches. I have encouraged the lower lines to become strong by allowing them pronounced extension growth to fatten them before trimming.

	1966	1967	1968	1969	1970	1971	1972
ROOT ESTABLISHMENT JAPAN	Grown in pot		Field grown				
TRUNK DEVELOPMENT JAPAN	Fed heavily in pot		Fed in field	Trunk chopped spring to mid season	Fed heavily in field		
BRANCH TRAINING JAPAN	NO TRAINING						
ROOT DEVELOPMENT JAPAN	Roots well spread for radial surface development			UNDISTURBED			

	1981	1982	1983
ROOT ESTABLISHMENT UK	Grown Training Pot	Transferred to larger pot	
TRUNK DEVELOPMENT	No appreciable thickening yet, but this will happen as the tree grows in the bigger pot selected in 1986		
BRANCH TRAINING UK	Each season the techniques of growing on, wiring, trimming, and spur pruning have been followed. The extension sought has been allowed to progress at 5 cm each year		
ROOT DEVELOPMENT UK	Consolidated in temporary pot	Transferred to larger pot with little disturbance	Consolidation enhanced by feeding
CHANGE OF POT	Dark grey unglazed oval 18″ × 13″ × 2½″ 46 × 33 × 6.5 cm	Off white glazed oval 20″ × 15″ × 2½″ 51 × 38 × 6.5 cm	

4. ROOT DEVELOPMENT

In 1973 the tree was probably dug round and lifted and a root ball preserved of say, four times the width of the trunk base. In 1978 the heavier and longer base and surface roots were trimmed short to encourage the beginnings of a root pad.

From the state of the roots on arrival, it was possible to deduce that the tree at most had been lifted not more than the conjectured two to three seasons from open field growth, as the roots were found to be of two

1973	1974	1975	1976	1977	1978	1979	1980
Trans-plant Field grown					Trans-plant Pot grown		
Trunk chopped suckers removed	Fed heavily in field	Minor trunk grafted			Trunk chopped suckers removed		
		Grown, wired, shoot trimmed, spur pruned each year					
Heavy root reduction		UNDISTURBED			Heavy root reduction	Feeder roots developed	

1984	1985	1986	1987	1988
Repotted into longer pot		Repotted into larger pot		
Roots combed and evened surface roots worked on	Consolidation enhanced by feeding	Roots combed and evened surface roots worked on		
Blue glazed oval 22″ × 13″ × 2″ 56 × 33 × 5 cm		Cream glazed oval 24″ × 16″ × 3½″ 61 × 41 × 8 cm		

types: logs and fine feeder roots! Hence the need to tie in, mentioned under Root Establishment, to encourage a pad to support the enormous lump of wood above.

The tree was transplanted into the off-white oval pot shown in the spur pruning sequence of autumn 1982, with minimal root disturbance to preserve the growing density of the pad.

The next repot was in spring 1984, into the blue oval pot shown in colour. At this time the roots were

Front view before
trimming, 1982

Side view before
trimming. Note the bulk
of the trunk

fully combed out and arranged with the fingers. New surface roots were noted developing from the original log-like field-grown surface roots.

The last repot was in spring 1986 into the much more capacious cream oval pot. The extra depth of this container helped the tree horticulturally by cooling the root with the greater reservoir effect available. At the same time it helped aesthetically, in that the former pot, being so much

Trimming progresses

Trimming complete.
Note how branch lines
appear firm as a result
of shortening back

shallower, had appeared to buckle where the heavy trunk form sat in it.

5. FUTURE EVOLUTION
I feel the Maple should be refined by maintaining the overall flattish profile through the branches, and by allowing the right lower limb more extension. By contrast, if the left-hand trunk area is kept compact, a very pleasant balance will be achieved.

TREE NO. 6

Mountain Maple Var: Yatsubusa Root Connected Style

Offering picture 1983. Yatsubusa Maple 53 cm (21 in) high × 101 cm (40 in) wide. 30 trunks. 35 years

1. ROOT ESTABLISHMENT

The group was imported in 1984 and planted in the irregularly formed, simulated stone container supplied with the tree. The effect was of a plant contained, but not really 'happily' planted. The tree did well horticulturally, quickly expanding its excellent, flat, dense root system. I had no other container big enough at that time to house the root system, otherwise there would have been no question of using the container supplied. The sandstone rock image implied by the ochre/purple finish was far too heavy for combination with the dainty, compact nature of the green foliage mass. It seemed obvious that a simple, light grey container, probably oval, was a better way to go.

2. TRUNK DEVELOPMENT

Some initial thinning was carried out *before* potting, observing the rule of interruption of the sap flow by trimming the root system first, before the branches and trunks. Because of the delicate size of each feature of this dwarf cultivar, great care was taken to seal each cut with Kiyonal.

In 1985 the same process was carried out to open spaces that the foreshortened angle had closed. In 1986 some overall thickening was noted. To avoid overdevelopment in the outer trunks where branch lines were being extended, some thinning of foliage kept these small and balanced.

3. BRANCH TRAINING

This aspect, along with root development and trunk development, was determined by the decision to sever the recumbent base at the two-thirds point. This enabled me to replant the resultant two sections as a disconnected 'V', thereby creating an avenue effect of the sort encountered when walking through a wood.

As soon as the two base sections were aligned, it became clear that to open the vista, some in-pointing branches had to be removed, and equally, some out-pointing branches had, in a lot of cases, to put on considerable extensions.

Complete group before cutting the trunk

	1984	1985	1986	1987
ROOT ESTABLISHMENT	Potted into container supplied	Repotted in spring Roots cut into two sections new pot	Repotted in spring Re-angled to increase perspective	▰▰▰▶
TRUNK DEVELOPMENT	Some trunks were removed before potting	Some trunks were removed when repotting	Some thickening noted	▰▰▰▰▰▶
BRANCH TRAINING	Some thinning before potting	Some thinning in summer after growth extension		▰▰▰▰▰▶
ROOT DEVELOPMENT	Pad good	Pad reduced and shaved to butt 'V' together	Light disturb-ance to increase acute angle	▰▰▰▶

Summer 1985. New
front. 25 trunks

With these factors in mind the foliage was thinned each summer to open and lighten the tiering between branch levels, and wired so extending lines could be placed precisely. Each branch plane was considered laterally and the profile of each tree was taken as a planed, natural form, with scale and balance dictating whether or not the planes and contours were in need of opening by pruning away, or building by pinching to increase density.

The summer picture of 1985 shows these techniques under way. The winter picture of 1986/87 shows the structure evolving along the new lines.

4. ROOT DEVELOPMENT

This was simplicity itself as the root mass was typical of that encountered with the dwarf Maples where the density of twigs, and branches is echoed in the extreme ramification of the roots. This density enabled me to cut and sculpt the root system safely in 1985 when I cut through the

Winter 1986/87

recumbent 'trunk' and cake-sliced the root mass to butt together the point of the 'V'. When I repotted in 1986 to increase the angle, in a year alone the root pad had almost magically grown together.

The tree is very strong, but the low winter temperatures of 1986/87 have left their mark on the tree through the small size of the current year foliage. To avoid damage in the future I plan to keep these dwarf cultivars warm footed, preserving enough temperature control to keep them frost free. Most finely branched and twigged trees are adversely affected by low temperatures as the tissue tends to dry.

5. FUTURE EVOLUTION

The planting needs a little more emphasis in terms of height at the left. It would be nice to see an increased extension to the lower left side and to the lower right.

These increases will enhance the perspective still further and give greater variety to the group.

After cutting, the group is now a 'V'

Right hand section

Left hand section

Rear view

TREE NO. 7
Trident Maple Informal Upright Style

The drawing above is of a famous Trident Maple that I have always admired. When I imported some heavy trunked Trident Maples I looked for one with a similar basic form and having found it, commissioned Gordon Duffett to make the pot.

The tree entered the UK in 1981. The branch system was built at the rate of 5 cm (2 in) per year in lateral spread. The annual extension was wire curved, trimmed, pruned and spur pruned. At each of these stages the tree was first permitted enough growth to gain the strength to react well to each process. The shoots were allowed to make four to five pairs of leaves before being treated and this minimized die-back in the winter and maintained tough, lively branches.

The feeding schedules for Stage I produced a strong tree that is rapidly approaching the outline of the original inspiration. I will now be switching to the feeding schedules for Stages II and III to preserve the detail in the design.

The reproduction exercise is fun to do and teaches one to look really closely at the structure of trees.

FUTURE EVOLUTION
In future seasons, the way to refine the tree and to make it closer to the original, is to spend a few hours scrutinizing the photo of the tree, branch by branch. This evaluating process teaches one to absorb the image. Then the fun comes from trying to marry the image and the tree itself.

Often, deep pruning will be necessary to give that precise change of direction, or perhaps only radical wiring can make the transition. The periphery will densen and the tree must be pruned, thinned and groomed to conform to the envisaged shape. The important thing is how much one learns about another artist's thinking in the process.

Summer 1985.
Trident Maple 73 cm
(29 in) high × 96 cm
(38 in) wide. Trunk
diameter 11 cm (4½ in).
19 years. Pot, white-
grey glazed rectangle,
58 cm × 40 cm × 12 cm
(23 in × 16 in × 5 in).

Summer 1985.
The same two weeks
later showing the
results of feeding and
the resultant luxu-
riance of well pinched
growth

STAGE II STRUCTURE AND FORM

TREE NO. 8

Mountain Maple Twin Trunk Style

Offering picture 1981. Mountain Maple
60 cm (24 in) high × 76 cm (30 in) wide. 40 years.
Trunk diameter 7.5 cm (3 in)

1. ROOT ESTABLISHMENT

The tree was imported in 1983. The root pad was excellent, very vigorous and with much fibre. The Japanese soil nucleus proved to be of red loam, so bearing in mind the soil/frost damage syndrome, I washed and picked off as much of the loam as I could. An initial root thinning sat the tree down into the flatter container chosen, a blue-green glazed oval, measuring 53 × 35 × 6 cm (21 × 14 × 2½ in), and a better image was created with the floating branch lines echoed in the lines of the pot.

2. TRUNK DEVELOPMENT

In the summer of 1984 I reformed the trunks by reducing their height by about one third, thereby removing a straight, log-like section (see photo sequence).

In subsequent seasons, balancing the trunks with branch cladding has created a more convincing trunk line in each case and one where the line flows. Some thickening is taking place and this has been monitored in the usual way by foliage thinning, to maintain trunk proportions.

3. BRANCH TRAINING

The major portion of branch training took place in summer 1984 when the trunks were reduced. The branches were flattened and spread with wire. The tree is vigorous and throws back buds quickly and consequently, as with all vigorous Maples, the branches constantly try to rise. Therefore tying down was and is necessary to maintain planed form. If you look at the two summer 1985 photographs, you will see how the branches have risen in the first, and have been swept down in the second through pruning and wiring.

4. ROOT DEVELOPMENT

The root nucleus on this tree is well formed and very strong. As the surface roots are visually supportive in a very satisfying way, I do not feel inclined to try and work on surfacing additional root lines.

Summer 1984
The head before
restructuring

Close-up of the head

Head shortened to
feature side branch as
new leader

Head restructured

Summer 1985

Summer 1985. Taken
ten minutes after the
last shot!

Tree restructured to
blend with new head

5. FUTURE EVOLUTION
I see the tree developing a rounded
head in the main, with the second
trunk echoing the form. The left
hand side at a distance would appear
deeply domed and the right hand
side, as a shallower, saucer-like form.

Every effort should be made to
lighten the form and preserve the open
spaces, as this tree buds profusely.

To help reverse the tendency of
this particular plant to produce heavy
apical growth, I would suggest that
low nitrogen feeds are used and that
perhaps water should be given
carefully rather than too liberally.
Both these factors will help to control
sappy, heavy top-growth.

	1983	1984	1985	1986	1987
ROOT ESTABLISHMENT	Some thinning of roots to fit flatter pot	▨	Repotted in spring	▨	Repotted in spring
TRUNK DEVELOPMENT		Trunks restructured in summer	SOME THICKENING ▨		
BRANCH TRAINING		Areas thinned and wired summer dewired autumn	Branches rewired in spring dewired autumn	▨	
ROOT DEVELOPMENT	Surface root nucleus good	▨			
CHANGE OF POT	Blue/green glazed oval 21″ × 14″ × 2½″ 53 × 35 × 6 cm	▨	Yellow/grey glazed rectangle 20″ × 15″ × 4″ 50 × 38 × 10 cm	▨	

STAGE II STRUCTURE AND FORM

TREE NO. 9

Trident Maple Informal Upright, Root Over Stone Style

Offering picture 1981. Trident Maple 50 cm (20 in) high, trunk diameter 7.5 cm (3 in). 60 years. Pot, dark brown unglazed oval, 46 cm × 33 cm × 6 cm (18 in × 13 in × 2½ in)

1. ROOT ESTABLISHMENT

The tree was imported in the winter of 1981/82. The root pad was excellent: well formed and dense. The soil composition in the root mass was 70 per cent sand and 30 per cent red soil. I used the oval container supplied and the tree grew happily planted in soil consisting of 70 per cent sand and 30 per cent mixed organic material (leaf mould, peat and pine bark). I repotted the tree in 1985 and found the roots to be excellent.

2. TRUNK DEVELOPMENT

There has been a slight thickening of diameter, but the main changes have been cosmetic, where branches have been removed to expose the trunk line. The deeper container used in 1985 acts as a good reservoir and root receptacle and has encouraged the trunk thickening which is now under way.

3. BRANCH TRAINING

The relationship of trunk and branches and in particular the 'natural' display of the branches and twigs, were what drew me to this tree. In leaf the tree became heavy, especially top heavy, so I decided to prune a few select branches. I worked over the basic divisions in the tree, beginning by greatly reducing the apical areas, taking away crowded knots of twigs to refine the branches. The charm of the tree lay for me in the way the upturned crests of rising layers broke across the basically vertical lines. I tried to enhance the individual character of each layered head by flattening it a little, pruning the centre to lower it and wiring the edges out sideways to increase the lateral flow. I phased this operation over the summers of 1984 and 1985. I foresee the lower right limb being extended.

4. ROOT DEVELOPMENT

The significant thing here is that the tree was not planted over the stone, but the stone was inserted under the main roots. There is little root to stone consolidation or webbing of the roots, as one can see in the case of tree no. 4. The situation could be

OPPOSITE:
Summer 1985

	1982	1983	1984	1985	1986	1987
ROOT ESTABLISHMENT	Potted in pot supplied			Repotted in spring		
TRUNK DEVELOPMENT	LITTLE CHANGE YET IN DIAMETER					
BRANCH TRAINING	Some continual shoot pruning		Branches thinned out and styled		Contours bulked with extra pinching	
ROOT DEVELOPMENT	LITTLE CHANGE				Use of moisture pad will enhance stone gripping	
CHANGE OF POT	Dark brown unglazed oval 18″ × 12″ × 3″ 45 × 30 × 7.5 cm			Dark brown unglazed rectangle 18″ × 13″ × 3½″ 45 × 34 × 8 cm		

improved if a moisture pad were placed over the roots to enhance their thickening. The pad could be formed from sphagnum moss and could be held in place with a plastic sheet clipped into the soil or bound round the stone.

5. FUTURE EVOLUTION

The pads of foliage might be considered in isolation, by inner pruning, to become almost like the crowns on several trees. This would be a logical progression based on the rising, spreading branch forms.

Visually, with the inner load thinned and extra extensions added, the tree will suddenly look much bigger. I think the current distribution of form is satisfactory, but with extra foliage bulk to play with, the potential nuances of shape and contour offered are endless.

TREE NO. 10
Trident Maple Raft Style

Photographed in 1975. 90 years. Trident Maple 30 cm
(12 in) high × 60 cm (24 in) wide. Pot, dark grey
unglazed oval, 53 cm × 38 cm × 8 cm
(21 in × 15 in × 3½ in).

1. ROOT ESTABLISHMENT

I acquired this tree in the winter of
1971. The tree was solidly established
in the original pot supplied from
Japan in 1966, which was a dark
brown unglazed rectangle measuring
53 × 25 × 5 cm (21 × 10 × 2 in). The
tree grew well in 1972, but was dryish
at the root so I decided to use a larger
pot in 1973. I selected a dark grey
unglazed oval measuring
53 × 38 × 8 cm (21 × 15 × 3½ in). The
tree soon settled after repotting and,
with the extra moisture and root run
available, it grew profusely.

In 1978 I imported an oval pot in
an unglazed oatmeal colour and
repotted the tree. The new container
measured 71 × 33 × 6 cm
(28 × 13 × 2½ in). The lighter image
and longer line suited the emerging
laterals in the tree.

In 1985 I decided to use a slightly
smaller but broader and deeper
container to enable me to turn the
major axis of the tree away from the
viewer. The extra moisture proved a
boon to the tree which grew profusely
once again, spurred by the extra root
run and reservoir action. The pot was
a light grey unglazed oval measuring
60 × 46 × 7.5 cm (24 × 18 × 3 in).

2. TRUNK DEVELOPMENT

In spring 1972 I repotted the tree and
reversed it to feature the present front
for the first time. I also tilted the tree,
raising the present front at the left
hand edge. This gave greater separ-
ation between the trunks and also
increased the perspective.

I achieved the initial banking by
mounding a mixture of peat, leaf
mould and sand under the tree. This
was soon thoroughly permeated by
root, and at each repotting I was
careful not to disturb this nucleus, with
the result it has now become a perman-
ent and natural feature of the plant.

The base trunk fattened steadily
between 1971 and 1985, but in the
last two years has increased in
diameter by at least 1.25 cm (0.5 in).
The bark has begun exfoliating and is
cracking up with the trunk expansion.
Note the close-up detail in winter
1986/87.

3. BRANCH TRAINING

When the tree entered the UK in

Summer 1977. 53 cm
high × 106 cm
(21 in × 42 in) wide.
Pot, dark grey
unglazed oval
53 cm × 38 cm × 8 cm
(21 in × 15 in × 3½ in).

Winter 1977/78

	1966	1967	1968	1969	1970	1971	1972	1973	1974	197...
ROOT ESTABLISHMENT	Established in original pot						Repot in spring			
TRUNK DEVELOPMENT	Little enhancement						Fattening noted			
BRANCH TRAINING	Good spur development						Each season branches extended, wired, pruned. Autumn spur pruned			
ROOT DEVELOPMENT	Steady thickening. Surface roots encouraged									
CHANGE OF POT	Original pot Dark brown unglazed rectangle 21" × 10" × 2" 53 × 25 × 5 cm							Dark grey unglazed oval 21" × 15" × 3½" 53 × 38 × 8 cm		

1966 most of the settled branching was lost due to very sloppy Japanese packing methods. The first British owner did very well to restart the branching, and the 1975 shot shows even so, how very tentative the new structures were.

To enhance the growth encouraged by the changes of pot I fed the tree heavily each season. I allowed the tree an initial three node shoot extension each year. This overall extension was wired and then allowed to grow away unchecked until the wires became tight. The wires were then removed and each emerging form was cut short, maybe back to two pairs of leaves, trying always to prune in such a way that the cut was made above a latent bud that would point re-growth in a pleasant direction. The resulting shoots were permitted to make two or three pairs of leaves before being cut short without wiring. This gave a pleasant mixture of curved and straight lines to the emerging branches. As growth consolidated with each season, I switched techniques and began taking side leaves and main shoots together each time I pinched, and this soon bulked out the contours.

I tried to flatten the lines of each branch by extending the underlines and keeping each crown shallow. Each autumn I spur pruned the branches short and sealed the cuts. Finally, after 21 years, the tree is beginning to find its true potential. I wonder how much sooner and better the result might have been if the original limbs had not been lost.

4. ROOT DEVELOPMENT
The base roots have tripled their size since 1966. Further surface roots are being encouraged and will add extra dimension to the beauty of the tree.

5. FUTURE EVOLUTION
I see the trunks as being featured more by lightening the foliage close in, making the foliage pads appear to spread further along existing lines. The interior thinning combined with still more extension will give a floating feeling.

1976	1977	1978	1979	1980	1981	1982	1983	1984	1985	1986	1987

Repot in spring

Repot in spring

Repot in spring

Rapid expansion

Each season branches were allowed minimal extension.
Shoot and side leaf removal technique for density

Oatmeal unglazed
oval
$28'' \times 13'' \times 2\frac{1}{2}''$
$71 \times 33 \times 6$ cm

Light grey unglazed
oval
$24'' \times 18'' \times 3''$
$60 \times 46 \times 7.5$ cm

Winter 1986/87

Summer 1986

Winter 1986/87. Close-up of trunk

TREE NO. 11

Mountain Maple Var: Kashima Upright Clump Style

Offering picture 1981. Kashima Maple 60 cm (24 in) high. Trunk diameter 7.5 cm (3 in). 35 years. Pot, grey/brown oval, 40 cm × 30 cm × 7.5 cm (16 in × 12 in × 3 in)

1. ROOT ESTABLISHMENT

The tree was imported in the winter of 1981 and was planted in the grey/brown oval pot supplied. The root system was excellent: dense, compact and with good surface roots. Once again, the soil nucleus was comprised of 70 per cent sand and 30 per cent red soil. I matched the soil mixture and after two months' growth it became obvious from the constant drying out that the tree would need a bigger container.

In spring 1983 I selected the oval pot shown in the summer 1986 picture. This immediately improved the general condition of the plant, affording the reservoir and root run needed to keep the roots cool and active. The amounts of foliage, as with tree no. 7, the other *Yatsubusa* cultivar, necessitate a constant exchange of water from the roots to offset that lost through the dense leaf mass. In spring 1986 I chose the soft-cornered rectangle shown with tree no. 8, as I fancied the *Kashima* in a narrower pot to enhance the mass of the tree, to make it appear bolder.

2. TRUNK DEVELOPMENT

Further trunks had been grafted into the root system at the lower left and the general taper was good. I monitored the trunk development by thinning the higher foliage areas to ensure the upper tree remained fragile and dainty. There has been an overall trunk diameter increase of 1.25 cm ($\frac{1}{2}$ in) in the last five years.

3. BRANCH TRAINING

Each summer I have trimmed away a proportion of the branches, beginning first at the apex and then working my way down the tree. If this is not carried out, the tree presents an unbroken wall of green and looks shrub-like.

In 1983, I removed some forward-facing branches that heavily masked the front, and also a percentage of the limbs that made the lower left of the tree too heavy. In 1984 I lightened the apex and thinned the foliage, removing climbing and descending details that cluttered the opened tiers. I was aiming at producing shallow domes of foliage with structured

	1982	1983	1984	1985	1986	1987
ROOT ESTABLISHMENT	Potted in the container supplied	Repotted in spring			Repotted in spring	
TRUNK DEVELOPMENT	Foliage monitored by thinning to preserve taper					
	Trunk diameter increased by $\frac{1}{2}$in/1.25 cm over the five year period					
BRANCH TRAINING	Each summer foliage was lightened					
		Some limbs removed	Apex lightened			
ROOT DEVELOPMENT	Surface roots good	Fine roots combed between to emphasise main surface roots			Fine roots combed to emphasise old and newer surface roots	
CHANGE OF POT	Grey/brown unglazed oval 16″ × 12″ × 3″ 40 × 30 × 7.5 cm	Cream glazed oval 24″ × 16″ × 3½″ 60 × 40 × 8 cm			Yellow/grey glazed rectangle 20″ × 15″ × 4″ 50 × 38 × 10 cm	

Close-up of the roots

Summer 1986. 68 cm (27 in)
high × 83 cm (33 in) spread.
Pot, cream glazed oval,
60 cm × 40 cm × 8 cm
(24 in × 16 in × 3½ in),
made by Gordon Duffett

Winter 1986/87. Yellow/grey
glazed rectangle
50 cm × 38 cm × 10 cm
(20 in × 15 in × 4 in) made by
Gordon Duffett

Close-up of the branches

lower lines showing here and there. In subsequent seasons I have let the tree produce a full weight of foliage and then I have reduced the bulk with fingers and scissors. Each zone has thereby been allowed first to build vigour before a reduction and, therefore, has soon budded back vigorously. To extend the lines where necessary, 5 cm (2 in) or so of lateral growth per year has been added.

4. ROOT DEVELOPMENT

The surface roots are good on this plant and I have tried to improve their appearance by combing between them at each repotting in order to emphasize their depth. Other surface roots are appearing and I foresee a tapering web formation in the future.

5. FUTURE EVOLUTION

I think the shifting visual weight of contour to the right of the main mass is satisfactory, but I would be happier seeing extra division between the tiers of foliage.

Perhaps to emphasize the extension of the lower right, some higher limbs might be shortened. If this was done to alternate branches the design would achieve greater variety and charm.

TREE NO. 12

Red Maple Var: Beniseigai Informal Upright Style

Offering picture 1970. Red Maple 63 cm (25 in) high, 7.5 cm (3 in) diameter trunk. 83 years. Pot, dark grey rectangle 46 cm × 33 cm × 12 cm (18 in × 13 in × 5 in)

1. ROOT ESTABLISHMENT

The tree was imported in the winter of 1970/71 and was planted in the dark grey rectangle shown in the black and white picture. It was noted that the soil used by the Japanese growers was about 70 per cent sand and 30 per cent red soil. Therefore much the same mix was prepared but with the addition of peat, leaf mould and a little loam. The analysis was around 70 per cent sand, 10 per cent peat, 15 per cent leaf mould, and 5 per cent loam. Much the same soil texture was aimed for, and as most of the existing mix in the root nucleus was in the 2–3 mm (0.08–0.12 in) granule size, a very well drained mixture was obtained. The tree was kept in a well-lit shed until it was safe to place it outside away from the frosts of May.

2. TRUNK DEVELOPMENT

The tree was planted into a 54 cm (21 in) oval pot in spring 1972 and this helped the branching to spread. Some surface root thickening was noticed. The tree was repotted in spring 1974 and again in spring 1976, but by this time trunk and root development were slowing down due to the pot being outgrown. A 76 cm (30 in) oval was used in spring 1978, and the tree grew strongly for two seasons and then slowed once more. The final container was the 95 cm (37 in) oval shown in the pictures from the mid 80s and the tree was transferred to this in spring 1980.

The form of the trunk is interesting: the root flare and trunk bole are magnificent and the trunk tapers to a point where the original leader was lost and a forward shoot was trained up. There is a cavity filled with fine cement where the tree was hollowed out after the loss of the leader. At a thickness of 10 cm (4 in) at a point well above the root flare, the trunk shows an increase of 2.5 cm (1 in) from the imported size of 7.5 cm (3 in) diameter. Although the trunk diameter has increased steadily throughout the 16 years since importation, it is true to say that the biggest increases occurred since the use of the 95 cm (37 in) pot, as this had the

Summer 1983. The late spring shoot mass before thinning and trimming back.

effect of underpinning the branch system with a large area of humidity, as well as acting as a larger reservoir and growing area for the roots.

The feed programme until 1980 was perhaps too meagre in an attempt to prevent over-strong top growth. Combined with the improvement in the growing conditions in the new

pot, the feeding schedule for Stage III has produced sound growth and rich colour.

3. BRANCH TRAINING

As the tree unfolded its magnificent spring colour for the first time, it soon became obvious that two things were going to happen: the tree would

soon overhang the pot unless vigorously pruned, and there would be the need for leaf thinning to balance the water available from the container in support of such a huge spread of soft foliage.

To preserve the basic structure of the branches in relation to the first, second, and even third pot, heavy branch pruning was necessary. Too heavy really—it became more like pollarding to fit the container—hence the choice of the really big pot with greater soil depth. Now the tree is assuming good form and the spread is easily maintained in relation to the limit of the pot.

By comparing the offering picture

Summer 1983. After thinning and trimming are completed. About 2 hours.

	1971	1972	1973	1974	1975	1976	1977
ROOT ESTABLISHMENT	Establish in Grey rectangle 18″ 46 cm	Transfer to Grey oval 21″ 54 cm	→	Repot spring	→	Repot spring	→
TRUNK DEVELOPMENT	3″ dia 7.5 cm	Slowish thickening Small pots and meagre diet inhibited development					
BRANCH TRAINING		Shoot trim, Large leaf trim		Branch prune at repot Shoot trim Large leaf trim		Branch prune at repot	
ROOT DISPLAY	Surface roots gradually exposed						

of 1970 with the recent pictures, you will see where I have removed large branches to lighten the form and to emphasize assymetry. The lower left original branch was far too low, and by removing it the planes were made interesting and the tree became more typical of the natural form of Maple which is to spread, rather than to sweep its limbs down like a pine.

The use of the high nitrogen feeds produces lush foliage and this must be handled vigorously. What I now do is to allow the tree to ramp a little, then I cut the excess and remove any large individual leaves any time they are produced. In general terms, I reduce shoot growth to one pair of leaves in the upper tree and allow it between two to four pairs of leaves in the lower areas. The effect of large leaf removal is to force smaller leaves and fine twigs, as axil buds are triggered. By the end of the season, leaves are tidy in size and long and heavy shoots are eliminated, but without the attendant stress that total leaf stripping causes. With such an old tree it is best to be flexible and to be technically responsive to its quirks.

I have grown the tree in several different locations but I now find that the best results are obtained when it is kept in well-lit, lightly humid surroundings, with good air flow. The trick is always to maintain protected conditions until the tree has produced its first set of leaves safely.

4. ROOT DEVELOPMENT
The bole and surface area were already well developed when the tree

1978	1979	1980	1981	1982	1983	1984	1985	1986	1987
Repot to brown oval 30" 76 cm		Repot to biscuit brown oval 37" 95 cm				Repot spring			
		Faster thickening / Adequate pot and feeding schedule / enhanced thickening rate						4" dia 10 cm	
Branch prune at repot		Branch severely pruned summer / Light trim	Shoot trim / Large leaf trim		Branch severely pruned summer / Light trim	Shoot trim / Large leaf trim		Branch selective removed summer / Light trim	

was imported. What I have done over the last 16 years is to expose more of the peripheral surface roots beyond the 25 cm (10 in) trunk base. There is scope for further careful work and a circumference of perhaps 46 cm (18 in) of radial surface roots would seem a not unreasonable support for such a full spreading tree. At each repotting the roots were thinned around the surfaced major roots to bring new growth nearer in.

5. FUTURE EVOLUTION

I see the tree as being pretty well settled in form. Detailed work in introducing more horizontal planes within the main masses would be nice.

The maintenance within such a frame is interesting. In the 1980 and 1984 seasons I used my 'paint-pruning' technique to identify coarse or busy branch areas in dormancy, and then to prune away the coded areas safely in mid season.

Nothing looks worse than a Maple with a tangled branch display, and always conscious of this, I have attempted to point the growth outwards and to remove all hanging areas below the strong main lines.

Usually, such heavy pruning, provided one uses the leaf trimming method outlined above, should not be necessary more than once in three or four seasons. When deep pruning, always try to enhance the form by choosing a shoot replacement that will create an interesting re-growth line.

Spring 1985. Red Maple now
stands 85 cm (33 in) high,
branch spread 120 cm (48 in),
trunk diameter 10 cm (4 in),
trunk bole 25 cm (10 in) at soil
surface. Pot, biscuit brown oval
95 cm × 46 cm × 8 cm
(37 in × 18 in × 3½ in).

Summer 1985

Winter 1986/87

TREE NO. 13

Trident Maple Informal Upright Style

Photographed in Summer 1977. Trident Maple 63 cm
(25 in) high. Trunk diameter 7.5 cm (3 in). 80 years.
Pot dark grey unglazed rectangle,
49 cm × 34 cm × 11 cm (19 in × 13 in × 4½ in)

1. ROOT ESTABLISHMENT

The tree was imported in 1970 and I acquired it in 1973. The root system was excellent, and when I repotted the tree in 1974, I mixed a lighter soil similar to the original 70 per cent sand and 30 per cent red loam mixture used by the Japanese grower. The roots were flat and dense and the tree soon grew rapidly after repotting and settled strongly into the new mixture. I have used similarly proportioned containers over the years as the pictures show.

2. TRUNK DEVELOPMENT

The trunk has increased slowly over the seventeen-year-period in the United Kingdom, due mainly to my policy of giving enough nitrogen to keep the foliage lively, but not enough to coarsen the growth of the branches. There has been an increase of 1.87 cm (0.75 in) in trunk diameter since 1970.

3. BRANCH TRAINING

Until 1984 this was largely a question of keeping the frame of mature and well shaped limbs within bounds. In the summer of 1984 I decided that the full rounded apex and adjacent areas were inhibiting the development of the lower tree and were also giving a round shouldered appearance to the tree. I cut away many main branches in the upper and middle tree to regain an overall tapered, triangular form. Compare the 1973 winter shot with that of winter 1986. In subsequent seasons I rebuilt the branch profiles and maintained the open character by thinning the foliage.

4. ROOT DEVELOPMENT

The surface roots were quite interesting but I have added others by digging around the main rootlines to feature side ramifications. This has often meant cutting away finer webbing to expose heavier material below. When I repotted the tree in 1974, a huge 'horse collar' of root ran round the container and this had lifted the root mass above the pot rim. I therefore felt it necessary to repot more frequently.

5. FUTURE EVOLUTION

I now see the tree as an essentially linear form or series of linear forms, rippling across the curving trunk. The flatter, broader domes seem to suit the branch frames better than the mounded profiles often seen with this species. In fact, I see the tree as being maybe a lighter edition of tree no. 12.

Winter 1973

	1970	1971	1972	1973	1974	1975	1976	1977	1978
ROOT ESTABLISHMENT	Potted in original pot				Repotted in spring				
TRUNK DEVELOPMENT	Slow increase in Trunk Diameter due to Low Nitrogen feed programme								
	Trunk has increased in diameter by $\frac{3}{4}''$/1.87 cm since 1970								
BRANCH	Maintenance pruning each season								
ROOT DEVELOPMENT	Additional roots surfaced								
CHANGE OF POT	Brown unglazed oval 21″ × 15″ × 3″ 53 × 38 × 7.5 cm				Dark grey unglazed rectangle 19″ × 13″ × 4½″ 44 × 34 × 11 cm				

Summer 1985. 81 cm high (32 in) × 96 cm (38 in) wide. Pot light grey unglazed oval, 58 cm × 44 cm × 8 cm (23 in × 17½ in × 3½ in)

1979	1980	1981	1982	1983	1984	1985	1986	1987

Repotted in spring

Repotted in spring

Repotted in spring

Main branches thinned in summer

Profiles rebuilt by pinching

Light grey unglazed oval
22″ × 16″ × 4″
56 × 41 × 10 cm

Light grey unglazed oval with rib
23″ × 17½″ × 3½″
58 × 44 × 8 cm

Winter 1986/87

Index